8 Weeks to a

Well-Behaved

Child

8 Weeks to a Well-Behaved Child

A Failsafe Program for Toddlers through Teens

James Windell

MACMILLAN • USA

MACMILLAN
A Simon & Schuster Macmillan Company
1633 Broadway
New York, NY 10019-6785

MACMILLAN is a registered trademark of Macmillan, Inc.

Library of Congress Cataloging-in-Publication Data

8 weeks to a well-behaved child : a failsafe program for toddlers through teens/James Windell

p. cm.

Includes index.

ISBN 0-02-630235-7   ISBN 0-02-860415-6 (pbk)

1. Discipline of children—United States.   2. Behavior modification—United States.   3. Child rearing—United States.

I. Title.   II. Title: Eight weeks to a well-behaved child.

HQ770.4.W558   1995

649'.64—dc20   95-5127   CIP

10   9   8   7   6   5   4

Printed in the United States of America

To Ellen

To all those parents attending my classes and seminars and who probably taught me more than I taught them.

Contents

Acknowledgments

There are a number of people to whom I owe gratitude for their contributions to my work with parents. First are the editors and management of The Oakland Press, published in Pontiac, Michigan, and in particular Bill Thomas, John Cusumano, Garry Gilbert, Dolly Moiseeff, Ginny Stolicker, Holly Shreve, and Julie Baumkel, all of whom have been helpful and kind in assisting in one way or another in my "Coping with Kids" column for the past several years. That column has given me a forum to express my thoughts on childrearing and to work out parenting and discipline ideas, while at the same time getting feedback from parents, children, and professionals.

Dee Dise and Rita Gray at Family Focus have helped me with parenting classes for Family Focus over a good many years. They have enthusiastically endorsed all of my ideas and directions for my classes. I've also enjoyed sharing ideas for my parenting classes with Vicci Salerno, a fine teacher in her own right.

I am also indebted to Dr. Barry Tigay and the staff at Oakland Psychological Clinic in Bloomfield Hills, Michigan, for providing a meeting room and referring parents to my parent-training seminars. I have been pleased that my colleagues have always been supportive enough of my efforts to entrust their clients to my Monday night classes.

I would also like to thank Dr. Pamela Howitt for asking me to set up and run the Parent Guidance training groups in the Intensive Probation Program at the Oakland County Juvenile Court. This experience has been exhilarating and has taught me a great deal about the strength and resources as well as the difficulties of parents of delinquents. John Chately in the Juvenile Court has likewise been a supporter of my classes and has furthered my interest in working with foster parents. I appreciate what he's done to help me.

There are several other friends and colleagues whom I would like to single out for their support and contributions to this book. Mary Pettit has always had time to talk to me about discipline issues and share her own experiences. Dr. Ismail Sendi gave me a chance to expand my skills with professional colleagues. The late Jeanette Morrison-Marks encouraged my work with children and let me learn from children and staff in her day-care center.

I very much appreciate the time and interest shown by my editor, Natalie Chapman, who always makes my manuscripts read more smoothly. And special thanks to my agent, Denise Marcil, who has made it possible for this book to be published.

I wish to thank my children, Jill and Jason, for their support and generous willingness to attend workshops and seminars with me, and my wife, Ellen, for her tolerance in sharing me with my computer so I could write another book.

And last, I couldn't forget the hundreds of parents who have participated in parenting groups, classes, and seminars, and who have contributed so much to my learning about parenting and discipline. Their questions and difficult parenting problems have forced me to continue to learn. A heartfelt thanks to you all.

Part I

Introduction to
Discipline and Children's
Behavior Problems

1.

What Can Parents Accomplish in 8 Weeks?

Can you change your child in 8 weeks?

Is it possible to reverse problem behavior in the space of two months? Will your child actually stop misbehaving that quickly?

And will you feel more competent and confident as a parent in just sixty days?

The answer to these questions is an unqualified yes. The purpose of this book, especially if you are frustrated, confused, perplexed, or at your wit's end, is to teach you a step-by-step method of dealing with your child. You *can* learn to deal more appropriately and effectively with your child's behavior problems in two months or less.

I have been helping mothers and fathers by teaching parent-training and discipline classes for some twenty-five years. Hundreds of parents I've met can testify that their children have changed and that they themselves have transformed their own abilities as parents in the space of 8 weeks or less in a class on how to use discipline. Whether the problem is a youngster who won't sleep in his or her own bed at night, a toddler who has violent tantrums, a child who is demanding and disrespectful, a boy or girl who fights with other children, or a teenager who has run away and has threatened suicide, parents find that they can bring about dramatic change in a few short weeks when they apply discipline techniques in new and effective ways.

The discipline skills and techniques that you will learn from this book are the same ones I teach in my classes. In fact, this book translates my 8-week program into written form, and follows the same approach I take in my class.

Week 1 of the course begins in Chapter 4, with each of the next seven chapters representing a new lesson. These eight chapters take you through the steps necessary to bring about changes in your child's behavior and to develop more effective parenting skills. In Week 1, you are introduced to the key elements that make parents more effective in raising competent and well-adjusted children. Also in the first week of the program, you learn to monitor your critical and negative remarks and to view your child in a different and more positive way.

There is a homework assignment given at the end of the first and each subsequent week. You are expected to do this assignment just as if you were attending the class. Practice is an important aspect of this program, because it is only through repetition of the skills that you can feel confident about understanding the concepts in the week's lesson and about applying them to your child.

In a book class, you are on your own. No one will be checking to see if your homework has been completed. However, if you are serious about making changes in your child, then it is essential for you to complete each assignment.

In Week 2, you learn the first discipline skill that you can apply to your child. It is Giving Praise and Attention, and it's the most fundamental technique that you will use to bring about positive change.

Week 3 teaches about Giving Rewards and Privileges. For parents worried about using bribes, this chapter explains the differences between helpful rewards and unhelpful bribes.

Week 4 describes another way of providing praise to children. It's called Using Reminder Praise, and is shown to be an effective addition to a parent's repertoire of skills. Also in Week 4 you learn about a 5-step method of increasing youngsters' compliance. This 5-step method ties together the two types of discipline techniques used as the basis for the entire 8-week program: discipline techniques to *encourage* desired and appropriate behavior and discipline techniques to *discourage* undesired and inappropriate behavior.

In Week 5, the first skill used to discourage misbehavior is introduced. This is Ignoring Behavior, and the dos and don'ts of using Ignoring as a parental discipline technique are discussed. Because Ignoring Behavior is so difficult for many parents, Week 5 also discusses steps to cope with stress that results when kids misbehave.

Week 6 tells about the factors that make punishment more—and less—effective. In addition, it introduces the use of Reprimands and Imposing Time-Outs as two more effective punishments.

In Week 7, the technique of Removing Rewards and Privileges is described in detail as a sound and useful punishment for both children and adolescents.

Finally, Week 8 rounds out the program by reviewing and summarizing what you have learned and showing how to integrate all of the techniques learned in the program when putting them into practice.

This 8-week class has been tested by me and other parent trainers who have used this program with thousands of parents. Like the mothers and fathers who attend my classes, you should find that this 8-week program gives you a grasp of the most important and useful discipline techniques you will need to employ with your child. When I talk to parents who have graduated from my classes, I find that they are always more self-confident and have a better understanding of what discipline skills they should use in various situations that come up with their children.

It may be helpful for you to know that these parenting skills and techniques are based on sound research principles and on the experience of numerous professionals who have worked with children and families. My own experiences with children and adolescents who have behavior disorders, and with their parents, have taught me a great deal about why behavior and conduct problems develop and how parents can solve them quickly and painlessly—particularly with children.

One of the most valuable lessons I have learned is that no matter how difficult the child or how ineffective the methods previously used by parents, the techniques given in the next several chapters will bring about important changes in the behavior of children.

Using Common Sense Correctly

There is nothing esoteric or mysterious about these methods. Some of the parents I work with often refer to them as "common-sense" discipline techniques. Other parents at first rather gleefully point out that they have used these strategies and techniques before, sometimes adding that "they didn't work."

They are right. They didn't work before. Not the way they used them. When I teach these techniques and approaches, I insist that parents follow certain rules:

1. Use the discipline techniques I recommend in exactly the way I tell you to. Take the time to learn the steps involved in each technique, not just the general idea. Only in this way can you be sure that you have indeed used discipline correctly.

2. Use discipline skills in combination with one another. That means that you can't take one discipline technique and begin using it by itself and hope to solve a child's behavior challenge. The right combination of discipline techniques, used in the proper way, often makes the difference.

3. Use recommended discipline consistently. This is difficult, and too often parents try for instant success with their children. Disciplining or punishing on one occasion will almost never solve a problem. Consistency—that is, using the right techniques in the right ways over a period of several weeks—is more likely to result in the kinds of behavior you want.

4. Use discipline with confidence. Too often, I have found, parents don't feel secure in using discipline. They convey this lack of confidence and resoluteness in the way they handle their kids' behavior difficulties. A tentative manner of handling children will do two things: a) It lets children know that they can continue to act irresponsibly because you are not sure enough about what you are doing to be authoritative; and b) It makes children anxious. When kids are anxious, they often act out their worries and anxiety, and one way of doing this is by misbehaving.

Either way, children who sense that their parents are insecure and tentative about what they are doing will not change. Instead, they may act worse, because they know (or have some unconscious intuition) that the rule or the discipline technique of the day—or the week or month—will soon change, and they don't have to heed it. Many parents are easily intimidated by their children simply because they are not sure of what they are doing. That's because most of us have not been trained in the use of discipline techniques. When we are unsure about ourselves, we are more likely to back down, give up, or just act timid and unconfident.

By studying the discipline techniques in the following chapters, you can use discipline like an expert. When parents use discipline confidently, when they are convinced that the methods will work, and when they persist in using the right discipline in the right way, the methods I recommend do work.

What Is the Discipline You'll Learn in This Book?

It may be helpful to define the word *discipline* as I use it in this book. To me, discipline is all the things you do as a parent to guide, direct, shape, and teach your children. Looked at in this way, discipline is all the ways you attempt to improve your child, teach your child right from wrong, and guide your child to be a decent and loving person.

When children are not loving, decent, and well-behaved, parents frequently become frustrated. Many parents read a book like this or enroll in a parenting class because they are baffled by a child's behavior problem. No matter what they've tried, this problem just won't go away. They try rewards, "bribes," lecturing, reasoning, punishment, or even spanking. Usually after a few attempts with one approach they abandon it to try another. This kind of "discipline shopping" serves only to confuse parents and make them less confident and much less sure of what to do with their children.

You may be skeptical about reversing a problem that has been going on for several weeks, months, or even years. Many parents are not easily convinced. And sometimes this skepticism about a quick change in a child's behavior problem has been fueled by a counselor or psychotherapist. One of the statements that counselors and therapists often use with parents concerned about a child's behavior problem is this: "Don't expect things to change overnight. After all, it took a long time for the problem to develop—it will take a long time to change it."

That's conventional wisdom. But it's not necessarily true. Although ineffective parental responses to a youngster's behavior may have caused or perpetuated the difficult behavior over several months or years, that doesn't always mean that we should have to wait several years for our children to change. Most of us feel we don't have that much time. We want quick results.

Although there is no eight-second cure, there are some shortcuts that many parenting experts now know work relatively rapidly.

My first class consisted of parents ordered by a juvenile court judge to attend parent-training sessions. I have little doubt now that I didn't know much about what I was doing twenty-five years ago, and I think the results of my classes showed that. I was thinking like a therapist and wanted parents to come up with their own answers and their own solutions. I wanted them to come to appreciate the subtleties of language and communication. I hoped they would adopt a democratic philosophy of childrearing. I expected to turn those reluctant, often resistant mothers and fathers of neglected and delinquent youngsters into junior therapists. Naturally enough, I failed rather badly.

Those parents taught me a lot. They taught me to change my methods and techniques. Over the years, as I have continued to lead parent-training classes and to counsel with a wide variety of parents both in and out of juvenile courts, I learned that I couldn't transform parents to think or act the way I would (or thought I would) in most discipline situations. What I could teach them was something far more valuable. I could teach them a repertoire of discipline skills and approaches to use like tools with their misbehaving children. Those tools could then be applied to a variety of situations. When parents needed to make a decision about how to handle problems in raising children, they could choose from the array of techniques they had learned. The end result would be that they would be more effective disciplinarians.

Over the past several years, while working with hundreds of families each year, I have gradually refined my approach so that it works with the great variety of parents who enroll in my classes. And along the way I have found methods to help parents bring about relatively quick changes in their children. Nearly every day I hear from parents who have used new approaches or more refined discipline methods to change their children. The results when parents develop more confidence and a wider repertoire of discipline skills are truly amazing. I am very proud of the many parents who have proved to be so adept at changing their approach to raising their children.

Success Stories

You may be interested in the kinds of 8-week wonders I have seen over the years. The parents I see the first week of my class are usually skeptical. Often they have been coerced into coming by a spouse or referred by a social agency or even ordered to attend by a juvenile court, family court, or divorce court. Their attitude is often: "Yeah, all of this is great, but I've got a kid who has serious problems. I need help now!" Or: "I don't see how my taking a class will change my child. She's got the problem, not me!"

Frequently the parents who come to my classes have "serious" child misbehavior problems. If they weren't serious, the parents wouldn't be upset or perplexed. Or the child wouldn't be on probation to the court. If the situation were easy, the parents could have solved it on their own without coming to a class. Once there, they are dubious about what they will get out of a class. One couple, Bernie and Rosie, came to one of my classes. They had a six-year-old son who was, in their words, "a holy terror." Mark, their son, was "the kind of kid the other parents didn't want their children to play with." He wouldn't listen, didn't mind his parents, was disrespectful to other adults, and had little self-control. At any meal he disregarded the family rules about eating, leaving the table frequently and stuffing food into his mouth. When playing with other children, he hit anyone who angered him. And he stole toys and other objects from other children's houses. During the first class, Bernie said he needed to learn to set up better structures and to "apply rules with consistency." He was hopeful that the class would help, but very tentative about expecting any real change. At the end of 8 weeks, Bernie and Rosie had lost all doubt. No longer was six-year-old Mark quite the problem he had been.

Both Bernie and Rosie were applying the consistent and firm discipline they had talked about wanting to use. What they said they learned to do in the class was to pay attention mostly to Mark's positive and approved behaviors while avoiding their previous critical remarks and punitive actions. They learned to ignore and stop reinforcing "bad" behaviors, and they found out how to tell Mark what they expected and to reinforce the desired consequences. All of this was done with assurance and confidence, which had the right effect on Mark. Mark was better behaved at dinner time and when he played with other children. He was even being invited to other children's houses because he could control himself better.

When Lori, the mother of four-year-old Wendy, started the

class, she expected maybe it would help a "little." But she certainly didn't see it changing the behavior patterns of her daughter, who came into her mother's bed every night and cried when Lori tried to make her sleep in her own bed. This routine had gone on for several months, and Lori had finally sought therapy about it.

Within two months, the problem was eliminated. Wendy slept in her own bed, Lori had her bed back, and there was no more crying at bedtime. "Every step of the program," Lori later said, "was important in changing the way I handled the situation. I saw that Wendy's unwillingness to sleep in her own bed had a lot to do with my feelings and the methods I tried to use with her. When I changed, Wendy changed. It was simple."

Sally had a sixteen-year-old daughter, Beverly, who had been in a juvenile institution for running away. Beverly was at home, but on probation to the juvenile court when the class began. Sally was certain that Beverly would violate her probation through more serious misbehavior and be returned by the court to a detention facility. They fought and argued incessantly. Rules were a big problem, and they often became intensely angry with each other.

"I don't know what I'm doing here," Sally said at the first session. "My daughter isn't going to change. She's the one who should be taking a class."

When the course was over, Sally saw things differently. "Beverly and I get along fine now. She does what I ask her and she comes home on time. We're really having fun for the first time in years. When I do have to punish her, she obeys. I can't believe the change in her."

Can it really be true that four- and five-year-old children start to listen and obey, long-established patterns of behavior shift, and sixteen-year-olds on probation to courts begin to be happier and more cooperative? In my experience it is true, and it has happened again and again. And the kids aren't in therapy, and they never attend one class. When parents begin to change their approaches to discipline, the change in children's behavior seems almost like a miracle to some of them.

The research and follow-up studies of the parents and families who have participated in my classes show the effectiveness of the program. Well over 90 percent of all parents report their children's behavior is improved. More than half say that there is "great" or "tremendous" improvement. Mothers and fathers say in response to questionnaires that they feel more confident about using discipline. And research results demonstrate that parents become more confident, hopeful, and aware of their ability to influence the behavior of their children.

In addition, tests given before and after the classes show that more communication begins to take place in the family, conflict between parents and kids diminishes, and parents feel as if they have more control in the family. Another important finding is that there is more warmth in the home atmosphere along with a changed perception of the former "problem child." At the end of the course, parents don't see their child as having great problems any longer, and they understand better their own role in handling whatever new problems or challenges may present themselves. No longer skeptical, doubtful, or hopeless about change, most become more optimistic.

The comments that parents write in response to questionnaires at the end of the 8-week program reflect what they have learned and the changes that, in their opinion, have taken place. These comments are as gratifying and meaningful as any statistics or research results:

"My child now knows more of what is expected."

"He is more open with me than he used to be."

"My kids respond faster and continue showing appropriate behavior."

"I was able to decrease talking back."

"My child is more attentive and acts more respectful to me."

"She doesn't even try to manipulate me anymore."

"We just took a long car ride last weekend, and there was actually peace in the car!"

"He is listening, going to bed without a problem, and getting ready for school without the old hassles."

* * *

When you finish reading and applying the methods proposed in this book, perhaps you will be able to say some of these same things. But your active participation and your sincere efforts to apply the steps and recommendations at the end of the chapters are required. No parent can expect to passively read a book and hope that a child will change. You will have to do your "homework." That, in fact, is the cornerstone of the methods described in this book.

Treat this book like a class you are attending, do the assignments faithfully, and you ought to be able to see results in the next 8 weeks.

Summary

If you follow the step-by-step method for handling children's misbehavior described in this book, you should find that in 8 weeks, significant changes are taking place in your child's behavior. In addition, you will feel more confident and competent while learning to deal more effectively with your child.

The methods outlined will work for you if you use them consistently and exactly as recommended.

2.

Why Do Children Develop

Behavior Problems?

It seems so simple to explain why a child has a behavior problem.

We see parents with their children and we immediately say, "Aha! Of course. No wonder that child cries and throws temper tantrums. The mother always gives in."

Or consider a three-year-old boy I know. Nathan's parents are divorced, and his father is said to be a drug dealer who keeps a gun around the house. Nathan visits his father every other weekend. It's "easy," therefore, to explain why Nathan is so aggressive with other children at day-care. "Of course, with a father like that, it's no wonder Nathan is so aggressive at school," a friend of the family said.

I also know an eleven-year-old boy who has no interest in school even though everyone says he is extremely bright. "It's simple to explain," a teacher commented about this boy. "His father pushes him too hard about getting a good education. No wonder he's turned off by school."

Then there are the children who whine, demand their own way, refuse to attend school, lie to their parents, run away from home, or resist being toilet trained. It requires little effort to look at the family environment and conclude, "Of course that child is doing those things. It's because the parents are . . ." And you can fill in the blanks to complete the judgmental conclusion: The parents are too lax, too harsh, too punitive, too inconsistent, too seldom home, too controlling. They have too high expectations, don't have high enough expectations, use bribes, don't use bribes, aren't supportive, are divorced, or always bail their kids out of jams.

It's easy to play the game of making instant analyses of behavior problems. Anybody, including professionals, can do it. The trouble is, simplistic diagnoses lead to simplistic treatments.

If we're concerned about change, it's more helpful for parents to learn more appropriate approaches to handling discipline, along with more effective techniques to greatly reduce or eliminate problem behaviors.

What is a behavior problem? It is any difficult behavior that causes parents concern and continues for more than a few days. A behavior problem can be as mild as a child's inability to sleep at night because of being afraid someone will break into the house, or as difficult as a child's stealing, running away, setting fires, or using illegal substances.

If you are dealing with a child or adolescent who has a difficult behavior problem, you don't have to blame yourself. But you should be aware of which children and teenagers are most at risk of exhibiting a behavior problem, the influence parents do have over their children's behavior, and the role of inborn characteristics and heredity.

Which Children Are at Risk for Behavior Problems?

Children are born with a variety of personality characteristics and temperament traits. When the combination of traits and characteristics makes a child more difficult to raise, the child is at a greater risk for developing behavior problems.

However, just being a difficult child alone will not necessarily result in behavior problems. Other important factors include the expectations parents have of their children, the amount and type of stress that families experience, the parenting and discipline skills parents possess, and the knowledge of child development and child psychology that parents bring to the job of raising children.

Therefore, parents who have difficult children, unrealistic expectations, major stresses, inadequate ability to discipline, and little information about child development are most at risk for having children with behavior problems.

The particular combination of all the factors determines how well a child is going to behave.

Raising children and understanding what makes them tick is not simple. But by examining each of the factors that can bring about behavior problems, you will be able to appreciate why so many young people have serious behavior problems and why, according to the National Center for Health Statistics, more than two out of four children (over 50 percent) between ages five and seventeen have behavior problems that challenge their parents at one time or another. That proportion jumps to three out of every four children (or 75 percent) when there has been a divorce or remarriage in the family.

Let's look at each of the factors.

Children with Difficult Temperaments

Children are more likely to develop behavior problems if they are born with difficult temperaments. As every parent of more than one child knows, each child is unique. Every youngster comes into the world with his or her own personal style and way of reacting to the world and other people.

Some children are docile and quiet. Others are very active—sometimes hyperactive. Some are intense, whereas others are low-key and imperturbable. Some handle changes and transitions well. Some react to every event with much emotion, as if it were of earth-shattering magnitude. Some give in easily; others are very persistent and stubborn.

The research done by Drs. Stella Chess and Alexander Thomas in their justifiably famous New York Longitudinal Study, in which they have followed 133 children and their parents since 1956, has given us greater knowledge about the temperaments of children. Chess and Thomas report that the temperaments of children are an enduring set of characteristics that are apparent throughout childhood and into adult life. Temperament traits remind us that children are not blank slates that enter the world ready to be shaped. Each child is unique even before the moment of birth. The particular characteristics of a child become very important factors in determining whether a child will be at risk for developing behavior or conduct problems.

The temperament traits that most influence how parents and other adults react to kids, according to some parenting experts (such as Richard Abidin, who developed the Parenting Stress Index in 1976), are adaptability, demandingness, mood, and overactivity. How a child handles change, how stubborn or compliant a child might be, how cheerful or whiny a child is, and how energetic or passive a child is will play a role in the way adults react to him or her.

A child who shows open defiance and demands a lot of attention will exert stress on parents. The overactive and highly distractible child is likewise a continuous drain on a parent's energy. Parents of such children must always be "on duty," vigilant and alert. Depending on how adaptable, demanding, moody, and overactive a child is, interactions between parent and child may be pleasant or unpleasant, positive or negative. A mother and father may feel close to a child or more distant, angry or anxious, depending on the constellation of these four traits in the child.

Many, if not most, of the parents with whom I have worked acknowledge that the child who presents the behavior problem was difficult from birth. They typically make this kind of remark: "He was headstrong right from the beginning" or "She was always stubborn and could never take no for an answer."

Let me give an example of how personality and temperament traits help to shape behavior problems.

Diagnosed as having Attention Deficit Hyperactivity Disorder (ADHD) by the age of three, Matt spent several months in a children's psychiatric institution before he was five because he was (in the words of his mother) "impossible to control." At nine years of age, he still has all the same characteristics that made him a difficult child to raise as a toddler and preschooler.

Matt is an intense child. He reacts strongly to everything and everyone. If he is not allowed to watch television before school, he may explode. When he sees his father after several hours' absence, he is initially hostile and demanding. It is not uncommon for him to act in what seem like very angry ways when he is in one of his "moods."

If it isn't his turn yet with a video game when playing with another boy, his way of responding is a quick outburst: "Give it to me!" When he feels he has been treated unjustly by a teacher, a parent, or another child, the whole world knows about it, because Matt never accepts anything quietly. He is upset at any slight. He wakes up from naps in a foul mood. He doesn't adjust well to changes, and even at age nine he may still cry about a change in his life.

With these kinds of temperament traits, Matt is a difficult boy to handle. No matter how his mother disciplines him, it doesn't seem to work. As a result, his mother and father often run out of patience with Matt and are frequently critical and punitive. Since he reacts strongly to injustice, he sees himself as being singled out for punishment.

Then there is Jonathan. A friendly ten-year-old with a compliant, docile demeanor, Jonathan elicits friendliness from adults. He accepts whatever happens with an easy-going manner and is usually even-tempered. Rarely does anyone criticize him or even threaten punishment. Jonathan seems to want all adults to like him, and they do.

If you have a Jonathan, you will use certain kinds of discipline. Actually, with a child like Jonathan, almost anything you do by way of discipline will work. It's hard to make a mistake with a docile, easy-to-raise child. The opposite is true with a child like

Matt. Almost any discipline you use will seem wrong and appear not to work. You will inevitably feel inadequate and frustrated. As a consequence, you will resort to more negative, critical remarks and almost always more severe punishment. Your attempts at reasoning will meet with abject failure. That kind of frustration often leads to more punishment, more attempts at coercion, and greater parental frustration, stress, and depression.

Which boy is most likely to end up with behavior problems?

I'm sure you're saying Matt, and with good reason. But Matt wasn't born to be "bad." He's not a bad seed, and he didn't inherit any particular criminal traits or "trouble-making" genes. He is more likely to have behavior problems for one reason: Matt will bring out the worst in parents and other adults. He will get lots of attention for his difficult behavior, and his parents (and teachers) will be forced to treat him in a different way.

In light of the inborn temperament traits of children, it is vital to know if we parents have any say at all about how our children behave.

The Influence of Parents on Children's Behavior

How much influence do parents have over how their children turn out? The answer is lots. Research has shown that parents of children with behavior problems have certain things in common.

For instance, parents of children with behavior and conduct problems tend to use ineffective discipline techniques, usually have deficiencies in their ability to monitor and supervise their children, and may be unpracticed at using effective problem-solving skills.

When mothers and fathers are indifferent to their children or are unable to track their kids' whereabouts, there is a greater chance those kids will get into trouble. If a child has broken a rule, parents who are unable to respond consistently or effectively are more likely to encounter continued troubled behavior from the child.

Researchers have also determined that how parents respond to aggressive behavior (which could mean hitting, pushing, and other antisocial actions directed at others) when it is first displayed is very important. This is particularly vital in the preschool years, when aggressive behaviors are usually first displayed. If parents use effective methods of discipline, then the aggression usually will not continue into later years. But if parents use coercive tactics—that is, threats, punishment, or force (even hitting)—to stop aggressive behavior, very often it continues or gets worse.

Studies by Diana Baumrind at the University of California at Berkeley found that children who were happy, self-reliant, and able to meet challenging situations directly tended to have parents who exercised a good deal of control and demanded responsible, independent behavior. Their parents were also more likely to explain, listen, and provide emotional support.

Parents do, in fact, have a profound effect on the behavior of their children. But the way a parent responds to children may be influenced by a concept called "Goodness of Fit."

First suggested by the work in temperament traits by Chess and Thomas, goodness of fit refers to how well the parent's traits and characteristics mesh with those of the child. When we understand and like (as opposed to "love") our child, we will tend to respond in a more understanding manner, usually with more empathy and patience. Some people seem to have a knack for raising children. This may be due to goodness of fit or personality characteristics that seem important for the task of raising children. For instance, a mother with lots of patience is likely to be a more effective and supportive parent than one who is usually impatient or short-tempered. A father with a tolerance for stress may well be a better parent than one who has a poor ability to withstand day-to-day stresses and pressures.

A sense of competence as a parent makes a difference, too. Usually we feel more competent if we understand and like our child and if he or she responds well to the discipline we use. However, one other aspect of feeling competent is how much investment we have in being a parent. Although we become parents for various reasons, the more seriously we approach the job and the more value we place on it, generally the bigger the commitment to being a good parent. With a commitment comes time and a great willingness to work at learning to be a good parent. Out of this work should come a greater sense of competence.

Other parent characteristics do play a part in raising children. How one is raised has a bearing on how expert one becomes as a parent. There is not, of course, a one-to-one correlation between having been raised by good, effective parents and becoming a loving, kind, effective, supportive mother or father. Plenty of parents who were raised in dysfunctional families have determined to do better than their own parents and succeeded admirably. On the other hand, there are mothers and fathers so crippled by cruelty, incest, deprivation, or other abuse that they have considerable difficulty overcoming those experiences to be the kind of parent they would like to be.

Many adults who long to be adequate, loving parents simply don't know how; they just were not exposed to parenting skills and techniques that trained them to deal with the various challenges and problems of raising children. A parent who illustrates this point is Jennifer Collins. At thirty-nine, she is self-centered, frequently angry with her teenage daughter, and likely to retreat from dealing with her by turning over discipline to her husband or to her mother-in-law.

When confronted by a problem, Jennifer often finds herself reacting like her own father, a self-centered and uninvolved man. She is critical, tries to induce guilt ("How can you do this to me? Haven't I been a good mother? Haven't I always given you everything you wanted?"), and makes ineffective efforts at reasoning. Her idea of reasoning is to keep talking to her daughter until the girl agrees to do things Jennifer's way. After each encounter or confrontation with her daughter, Jennifer can recall a similar episode with her own mother or father. They handled things in the same way. "I promise myself to do things in a different way," Jennifer has said, "but when something goes wrong I always say the things I heard coming out of my mother or father's mouth. That makes me really angry with myself after I do it. But then it's too late."

Depression and Other Parental Problems Can Lead to Children's Behavior Problems

There are a few other parental factors that relate to the potential development of behavior problems in children. These are mental illness, physical illness, and depression in parents.

Mentally ill parents may not have the ability to withstand stress and challenges, and mild oppositional behavior by children may overwhelm them. When they are stressed too much, they may resort to behavior that is inappropriate or not at all what they would do in more stable situations. Parents who abuse or severely mistreat children may not be unloving, but may be psychologically and emotionally unable to provide the kinds of consistent parenting skills children need.

Yolanda Browne is an illustration of such a parent. Now in her early thirties, she agreed after a divorce to allow her two children, Hector and Victoria, to live with their father. Her reasons seemed to make some sense. Their father was in a better financial position to provide for the children. But Yolanda fully planned on visiting the children regularly. That's the way it was supposed to work. But something always seems to get in the way. One time it's car trouble, another time a fight with her boyfriend. Yolanda has been arrested, fired from her job, and forced to move from her apartment. Things are always going wrong in her life. People pick on her, there is a "conspiracy" by her children's father to deprive the children of her companionship, and the Friend of the Court is "prejudiced" against working mothers. Yolanda is never to blame, at least not from her point of view. If she hasn't seen her children in three months, it's not her fault. If only people would see her for the good mother she is, then her children could spend more time with her.

In fact, Yolanda has so many problems of her own that she cannot possibly concentrate on having a consistent visitation schedule. Because of her own childhood, with a paranoid and sick mother and a harsh, rejecting father, Yolanda has developed severe personality problems. Her emotional troubles seriously interfere with her ability to raise children. Her children tend to personalize her failure to show up, and her son, Hector, acts angrily and aggressively at times—very likely in response to the lack of consistency on the part of his mother.

Mothers and fathers who are depressed, research has found, are at risk as effective parents. We know that following a separation or divorce, for instance, the ability of both mothers and fathers often diminishes for the first one or two years. Other research indicates that parents who are depressed are more inclined to perceive their children as having greater problems, and to have children with behavior and adjustment difficulties. A depressed parent cannot have the energy, the patience, the tolerance, or the ability to think through situations.

Physical illnesses of all sorts may interfere with the ability to be an effective parent. A mother with muscular dystrophy, for instance, or a father with emphysema, may lack the energy and patience to deal with a compliant and generally obedient child, let alone a temperamentally difficult youngster.

Stress and Lack of Competent Discipline Skills Can Lead to Children's Behavior Problems

When parents lack competent discipline skills, either because they have not been taught how to deal with children well or because of stress, they will often deal with their children inadequately. The children, then, are at risk for developing behavior problems.

Indeed, when the level of any kind of stress is high and the stress is ongoing, the parents may be preoccupied with relieving that stress rather than trying to handle the many psychological needs of a child, including adequate discipline.

Parents who handle stress well are often more patient and understanding with their children or are more willing to take the time to reason with them. Stresses that can interfere with raising children are financial difficulties, marital problems, conflicts between parents over discipline or childrearing approaches, job pressures, and conflicts with relatives.

These stresses compound. During the first twelve months or so following a divorce, for instance, both mothers and fathers have been found to be more anxious, depressed, angry, and self-doubting. Parents who were competent and effective prior to a separation or a divorce cannot, during the one or two years needed for readjustment, provide the kind of loving and supportive discipline children need (particularly when they, too, are going through a rough time). Divorced parents tend to make fewer demands on their kids, often show them less affection, communicate less well with them, and are less consistent in their discipline.

How much stress parents display also seems to have a lot to do with how good or poor their relationship with their own parents is, and whether they have a support system. A support system could be a strong relationship with one's own parents, or a network of spouse, friends, and acquaintances who can provide encouragement and help in times of need. The tremendous growth of support groups in this country strongly suggests the need of individuals to find a sympathetic network of others who will shore up sagging spirits and low morale, or provide knowledge and insight into problems. Parents certainly need this as much as anyone.

Lack of Understanding of Child Development Contributes to Childhood Behavior Problems

When the factors just discussed—parental depression, high parental stress caused by family problems, and so on—combine with a poor understanding of child development and child discipline skills, the stage is set for a potentially troubled situation. That is, a child brought up in such a set of circumstances may be at considerable risk for developing behavior problems.

Many researchers believe that accurate and appropriate expectations for children's behavior are key to rearing young children well. In families where children do not develop well, experts suggest that less effective parenting is due not only to a lack of skill but also to a lack of knowledge about development. An important part of becoming a good parent is to acquire information about how children grow and develop in body, mind, and spirit. In addition to the information gained, the act of learning itself motivates parents to interact better with their children.

When parents know more about children's development, they can more skillfully design a supportive learning environment and interact with their kids in ways that stimulate a young child's development. Knowing how children develop also leads to more realistic expectations. When a child is born, parents have dreams, hopes, and expectations for him or her. We may want a child to be happy and well adjusted, to be popular, athletic, scholarly, or rich. We may hope he or she becomes famous, goes into a special career, or just turns out to be honest and hard-working with impeccable integrity. And sometimes parents expect their child to be rebellious, a hell-raiser, or a nonconformist. Or to be loving and dependent on us as parents, close to the family, handsome, beautiful, and graceful.

What we get may be what we wanted and expected—or it may be quite different. If our child meets our expectations (and this becomes apparent in many respects during the preschool years, when personality and temperament come into sharper relief), then we may be quite pleased with our child. When we are pleased, it's easier to be loving and affectionate. When they don't quite measure up to what we expected, we are often—at least secretly—disappointed. That, too, may well influence how we treat our child. Our reactions, whether warm or cold, rejecting or accepting, will reflect our feeling or belief that a child does or doesn't live up to what we expected. Having realistic expectations depends, to a large degree, on knowing about how children develop.

Parents frequently have children without knowing much about child development. For example, Susan Burke had a child at age eighteen. Before having Bobby, an energetic boy, Susan had never taken a class in child development and had not had the benefit of a child-care course, which is offered in some high schools. In fact, she had not even had baby-sitting jobs because she didn't like being around little children.

Susan grew up as an only child with parents who were in their forties when Susan was born. She was raised as much by her grandparents and an aunt as by her mother. Without younger siblings, Susan did not get to see how children are raised or to participate in their raising. As a young mother, Susan tended to be frightened and bewildered by the task of parenting. She was never quite sure how to read Bobby's signals, so common infant behaviors such as crying, refusing food, and nighttime waking provoked anxiety and insecurity in Susan.

As Bobby got older, and his behavior became somewhat more complex, Susan always seemed at a loss to respond appropriately to his behaviors. When he began walking and getting into more things at home, Susan tried in rather crude ways to train him. Often she was too harsh and was reported to a social services agency for child abuse. Later, as Bobby became more difficult for her to handle, she was cited for child cruelty and ordered to attend parent training classes.

When Susan showed up for a parenting class, she volunteered that she had never read either a discipline or a child development book. "I thought I would learn about Bobby as he grew. I didn't know you had to study this stuff," she said.

Without knowledge and good information about child development, Susan did not respond well to Bobby, even though she felt love for the boy. Over a period of several years and numerous "wrong" responses to his behavior and actions, Bobby had become a much more difficult-to-raise child than he should have been.

A Combination of Factors Can Lead to Children's Problems

While Susan Burke simply lacked information about child behavior and appropriate parental responses, there are other families in which a combination of factors produces a child at considerable risk for developing behavior problems. A family that illustrates this is the Collinghams.

Justin Collingham was a teenager who had grown up with two hard-working parents. But by the time he was fourteen years old, Justin was running away, stealing from his parents, and using illicit drugs and alcohol. The factors that made him what he became were there from the beginning. His parents, Peter and Christine Collingham, were married as teenagers. Christine grew up with a permissive mother and an uninvolved but punitive father. When Justin was born, Christine wished to be closer to him than either of her parents were to her, and she made this a major priority as she raised him.

She determined that she wouldn't punish Justin as she had been punished; she would be loving and close. Yet she and her young husband clashed about childrearing philosophies, so she took to protecting Justin from Peter as soon as Justin was a toddler and able to get around. While trying simultaneously to be close and protective and to avoid being a punitive parent, she became a very permissive parent who always had excuses for Justin's behavior.

Neither she nor her husband, both teenagers when Justin was born, knew much about what to expect from children or how to handle an active and persistent preschooler like Justin. The Collinghams frequently fought over each other's handling of Justin. Peter Collingham began to regard Justin as the property of his wife and would spitefully spank him when Christine wasn't around. Justin could therefore play one parent against the other. He recognized at an early age that his mother would take his side against his father (or anyone else) and that he could thereby avoid accepting responsibility for his behavior. Justin had a built-in excuse, also, because he was overactive, persistent, and very distractible. He learned to view himself as a "hyperactive kid" who was picked on by his teachers and father.

If Justin's parents had had more information and knowledge about child development when raising him, if they had been able to sort out some of their own stresses and individual differences related to rearing children, if they had known more about temperament problems and been able to accept him as the unique person he was; then they may have had a chance to discipline him in such a way as to avoid the acting-out problems he developed. Given his temperament traits, his parents' reactions to him, the stresses in the family over childrearing, and his mother's frequent depressive reactions to the almost constant marital problems, Justin developed a serious behavior problem. When his parents came for help, they recognized quickly how overwhelming the whole prospect of making major changes in the family would be.

Because Justin had a well-established pattern of acting-out behavior, much attention was paid to his misdeeds. If it wasn't his mother talking and "reasoning" with Justin, it was his father lecturing him about how "you're going to have to change your attitude if you expect to get anywhere in this world" or threatening to send him to the juvenile center. Most of the interaction between Justin and his parents centered around his most recent misbehavior.

In a family in which a combination of factors like those facing the Collinghams have taken root, young people are at risk to develop behavior problems. Not one factor in itself will necessarily lead to a misbehaving child, but when the factors begin to combine with one another, they usually have an impact on the behavior of children.

When behavior problems persist without adequate intervention by parents, they can become worse and may result in the kind of conduct problems that typically overwhelm and frighten parents.

There is one other factor that seems essential for a behavior problem to continue: Parents must pay a lot of attention to the problem. By being critical, acting punitively, or constantly harping on the misbehavior, the parents reinforce it. This aspect of children's behavior problems will be discussed more in Chapter 4 ("Week 1: The 12 Keys to Effective Parenting").

Summary

Children are at greater risk for developing behavior problems with the occurrence of one or more of the following factors:

1. The unique traits and characteristics of the child that make that child difficult to discipline.
2. Unrealistic parental expectations for children.
3. Parental stresses and pressures, depression, and other problems.
4. Lack of competent and adequate discipline skills.
5. Parents' lack of knowledge about child development.

3.

Why Traditional Methods of Discipline Don't Work Today

A man in my parent-training course sat in the back of the room. He scowled through the first several sessions, but he gradually moved closer, week by week. By Week 5, he was only a few chairs away from me, and he was obviously ready to ask a question.

"The trouble with kids today," he began, "is that they get away with things. When I was growing up, I wouldn't think of doing some of the things kids do today. Don't you think it's time we got back to traditional ways of raising children?"

Several heads in the audience nodded in agreement.

"If by traditional methods of childrearing," I said in response, "you mean being firm, consistent, and loving, then I couldn't agree with you more.

"But, if you mean that we should scare kids into being good, threaten them, or use physical punishment, then you and I have very different views."

Many people believe that as a society we have been much too permissive with our children for several decades. This may well be true. I believe it is true. And I put some blame on the mental health profession for confusing the public (and itself) on this issue.

But it is this same mental health profession—and the parenting experts, child development specialists, and others who have researched childrearing—that has led us to learn more about what makes for healthy and effective parenting.

Little or nothing about the "traditional" ways of raising children has any relevance for contemporary parents. If this sounds like a strong and opinionated statement, I mean it to be so.

Make no mistake, if you look at the history of childrearing in the United States as well as in other countries, it is apparent that children have been misused and abused for centuries. Several recent books that detail the history of childrearing methods document this. Among them are *Spare the Child: The Religious Roots of Punishment and the Psychological Impact of Physical Abuse* by Philip Greven, and *Reading, Writing, and the Hickory Stick: The Appalling Story of Physical and Psychological Abuse in American Schools* by Irwin A. Hyman.

For many people who advocate a return to more traditional ways of childrearing, it is essential to ask: To which traditional ways of childrearing should we return? In her important textbook *Social Development: Psychological Growth and the Parent-Child Relationship*, Dr. Eleanor E. Maccoby wrote that up to the seventeenth and eighteenth centuries in the United States and Europe, many—perhaps most—children were "victims of parental abuse." Philip Greven, in his book *Spare the Child,* recites personal accounts from people who grew up in the eighteenth century and told of physical punishment and discipline beginning before the age of twelve months. Is that the tradition we want to go back to?

Or is it the tradition in England two hundred to three hundred years ago when children were frequently beaten at home and school for errors and infractions of rules? Or when John Calvin stated that children who made a habit of disobeying their parents should be put to death? Or the times in the Industrial Revolution when children were forced to beg on the streets and work long hours in dirty factories?

I hear many people advocating a return to traditional methods of punishment with children, but never does someone in an audience (or in my office) suggest we return to a "glorious past" when it was okay to physically abuse women. Apparently, we have attained enough sophistication to assert (although not always practice) that it is not acceptable to abuse women, but we are still struggling with the issue of how to deal with children.

Philip Greven wrote:

> Most of us instinctively defend the practice of corporal punishment, partly out of loyalty to our own parents and grandparents, partly out of anxiety about ourselves (especially if we as parents have used physical punishment in rearing and disciplining our own children, as most of us have), and partly out of unwillingness to think that something so common and so ordinary could be so consequential and so damaging to so many of us.

It is this almost instinctive need to defend a way of dealing with children that suggests that we have become defensive about the harsher ways of disciplining children.

Today the discipline of children is in a transitional stage. Thirty states still allow physical punishment in schools, although twenty have banned it by law. In Michigan, as well as in a number of other states, licensed foster care parents cannot use physical punishment with foster children or their own children.

The transition is from a corporal punishment–oriented society to one in which parents use kinder, more thoughtful, and more psychologically appropriate methods of discipline. But as with any societal transition, there is uncertainty and confusion. Parents have a sense that they ought to be doing something different, yet they aren't sure what. The question they ask is: If I can't use traditional methods, what am I supposed to do to make my child mind?

That is the point of this book. We now know too much about how to raise children in healthy ways to return to methods of the past. There are more contemporary methods of discipline available, and they do work. The problem for a great number of parents, though, is that they were raised with "traditional methods of discipline," and that's all they know.

Confusing Firmness with Harshness

I was sitting in a group with several mothers recently when one woman asked what she could do to convince her husband that some of the discipline techniques I was teaching would work better with their children than the ones they had always relied on. She herself could see that since she had begun using alternative discipline skills, her children were more compliant and she had a better relationship with them.

"But my husband," she complained, "still threatens them and still thinks he can hit them and get them to mind." Several of the other women chimed in.

"I know what you mean," said a woman who was married for the second time. "My husband says that's the way he was raised, and he didn't turn out so bad."

"Yeah," echoed a single mother. "I'm not getting married again. I think all men think they can get kids to mind by being bigger, stronger, and tougher."

Many parents—and not just fathers—come to a parenting class like the scowling man who said he thought we are too soft on children. Such parents genuinely want to learn more. But their bias, more often than not, is on the side of strict and tough discipline.

One reason for this is the confusion people have over the meaning of being "firm" and being "loving." Many parents perceive a conflict between the two; they can't be both loving and firm. Firmness to them is equated with being mean, harsh, strict, and punitive. Love is the opposite. Showing love means being soft, quiet, lax, permissive, accepting, and a pushover. And, of course, this is where many couples encounter conflict in raising their children. If the father believes in being strict, the mother sees him as too harsh and punitive. If she believes that a parent should discipline with love, he sees her as weak and overly permissive. (Sometimes the roles are reversed, but the conflict is the same.)

Lacking an understanding of how parents can be both firm and loving, many parents of today's children—especially those whose own parents raised them in a more punitive and harsh manner—resort to the familiar coercive, threatening, guilt-inducing methods to bring about compliance. And their cop-out retort to anyone's efforts to change them is: "That's what kids need. That's what they did to me, and I didn't turn out so bad, did I?" No, perhaps you didn't turn out so bad. But maybe you could have been treated more kindly and still learned how to behave.

One of the benefits of research in the fields of child development, child psychology, and discipline over the past thirty to forty years is that we know so much more about what makes children tick and how they ought to be treated to bring about maximum psychological growth and development.

We know that children begin perceiving and learning literally from the first week of life and that how we teach them, love them, touch them, and respond to them will have an important effect on their emotional and psychological development.

With the advances in our understanding of children comes greater information about what discipline works well with children—not just to get compliance, but to teach them, guide them, and help them to grow up to be psychologically healthy.

Unfortunately, the actual treatment of children has not changed much—not just over the past few decades but over the past two centuries. There is a gap between what we say children need and what we (meaning a statistically large number of parents) do with our children on a day-to-day basis.

Recently, a father of a thirteen-year-old boy who has been called "incorrigible" told me how he got angry with his disobedient son. In a heated exchange, he hit his son in the shoulder and pushed him against a door so hard the boy lost his balance and fell into a heap on the floor. The father was hard-pressed to explain why his son ran away from home.

A single mother in a parent-training group told how she got so upset with her teenage son for refusing to study and getting unacceptable grades that she screamed at him that he was an "ignoramus" and slapped him twice.

These stories aren't unique to me or the parents with whom I work. Most social workers, child psychologists, and school teachers and counselors could confirm that such incidents happen in many homes—and in what are otherwise "good families"—with depressing frequency.

Despite what we know about the best ways to raise children, and despite the fact that parenting experts have been advising against corporal punishment for generations, child mistreatment and mismanagement continue. In fact, if you examine child abuse statistics in the United States over the past ten to fifteen years, you'll find a gradual increase in the number of reported cases. From the mid-1970s to the late 1980s, reported child-abuse cases increased from about 600,000 a year to around 2 million a year. This increase may represent improved methods of collecting data and greater public awareness of a shameful problem, but it also suggests that a great number of children are still mistreated, both physically and emotionally. And these numbers indicate only confirmed cases. They don't reflect the angry father hitting his son in the shoulder or the stressed mother slapping her boy for poor grades. Such situations don't become part of the statistics because no one turns these parents in to social service agencies that work with abusive parents. Many researchers in the field of family violence believe that the incidence of violence within families is dramatically underestimated.

It is very easy for many parents to think of the child-abusing parent to be the "other guy" and not themselves. Neglectful parents, we like to think, are the ones who leave their child home alone, or have an incestuous relationship, or beat a child with an instrument, or starve a child in a dark cellar. It is also comforting to think of the abusive parent as one who is maladjusted and deeply disturbed. Yet that's not what experts in the field have found.

The Kinds of Parents Who Use Harshness

There is no typical abusive "personality," but there are some characteristics that are frequently found in parents who carry "discipline" to the extremes. Such parents have limited knowledge of childrearing, experience considerable stress, have lower tolerance for common childhood behavior (such as crying), and lack accurate insight into why children misbehave.

This all means that parents who are unable to deal with stress in their lives, do not understand children, and have been subjected to family violence themselves may be the parents who resort to violence against children.

And many such parents justify their cruelty and place the blame for the misbehavior on children or young people by invoking the good old days of "traditional" childrearing. To the extent that "traditional" means "harshly punitive," there is no traditional method of childrearing to which we can or should return. The art of raising children well has been steadily evolving into a set of guidelines and practices that are now backed up by several decades of research. While there are many styles, approaches, or specific techniques that can lead to well-behaved and fairly well-adjusted children and young people, there are a variety of parental practices that should be discouraged.

Today we know very well what the risk factors are for producing maladjusted, behaviorally disordered children. These risk factors (the ones related to parenting, that is—there are others related to other aspects of children and families) are:

- Harsh parenting
- Inconsistent parenting
- Parental lack of supervision and monitoring of children
- Little positive parental involvement with child
- Parents engaging in antisocial behaviors
- Parents having marital conflict

In childrearing, if not in everything else in life, a return to the good old days is unwarranted and will not result in beneficial childrearing practices for children. There is no way that more harsh, punitive, inconsistent, and nonpsychologically oriented methods will ever produce healthy and well-adjusted children.

Summary

Although many people call for a return to traditional forms of discipline, there is little in traditional ways of raising children that is relevant to today's parents.

Parents frequently confuse firmness and harshness, and many wonder what discipline they are supposed to use if they can't or shouldn't use more punishment-oriented or physical means of discipine.

Children who are raised with harsh and inconsistent parenting, whose parents fail to supervise them, and who are not positively involved with their parents are at risk of being poorly adjusted and having behavior problems.

This book is an 8-week course that teaches parents how to deal with children in more loving, humane, and yet effective ways.

Part II

The 8-Week Program to Change Children's Behavior

4.

Week 1: The 12 Keys to Effective Parenting

This is Week 1, and you're ready to get started to make changes in your child. To begin—as I tell the parents who come to my classes—there are some things you need to know at the outset.

This is an 8-week program, and as such it has been designed to be followed in a certain sequence, with a curriculum that builds on what is taught each week. That means that you can't read just those chapters you want to read and skip others. They should all be read, and in order.

The class teaches a variety of discipline techniques that will better prepare you to understand and handle your child. Each week, starting with the second session, at least one new discipline technique is introduced, explained, and illustrated. At the end of the course, you will know several new techniques (or if they are not new to you, you will have been reintroduced to them, told how to use them most effectively, and reminded of their importance in dealing with your child) that will make you a more skilled parent.

Accompanying each week's lesson is a summary of the most important points taught, along with a homework assignment. To get the most out of the class, you will have to do each assignment, and that necessarily means practicing the techniques with your child. Each week, beginning with Week 2, my classes usually start with a brief discussion of the experiences parents have had practicing the homework given to them. If you have done your homework, you will better understand some of the comments made at the start of each succeeding chapter.

By reading the next eight chapters in the proper order, following the comments and discussions about each discipline technique, and practicing each assignment, you will reap the most benefit from this 8-week course.

Now, with that explained, you are ready to begin. We start with the keys to being an effective parent.

The 12 Keys to Effective Parenting

If as a parent you have a basic understanding of key parenting and discipline principles, you can apply what you know about effective discipline to your daily handling of your child.

When a new parent-training course begins, I ask the parents to name the key elements that constitute effective discipline. Usually some fairly good ideas emerge. But never in any of my hundreds of classes have I encountered a parent who could name as many as five or six concepts that make for effective discipline. Typical answers will include such concepts as love, trust, and communication. Someone will say either consistency or follow-through.

All of these are good ideas, and some are certainly vital to discipline. But the basic elements of effective parenting go further:

- Providing love, affection, and concern
- Helping children build self-esteem
- Having respect for children
- Accepting children and showing approval
- Having a good understanding of discipline techniques
- Providing clear and reasonable expectations
- Being consistent in handling children
- Setting strict and firm limits

- Having consistent parenting approaches among all the child-care figures in the home
- Enforcing limits
- Allowing dissent and expression of feelings within the limits
- Being able to let go of our children

All of these 12 Keys to Effective Parenting will be touched on in the next chapters because they are so critical to the sound raising of children. However, I will begin by commenting on just two of them in this chapter.

Providing Love, Affection, and Concern

There is no more essential aspect of competent parenting than providing generous amounts of love and affection. In fact, if you can't establish a warm and loving atmosphere, most of your discipline isn't going to work very well. This is especially true of punishment, which cannot be effective in a hostile atmosphere.

Establishing a loving and affectionate relationship as well as a warm, caring, protective, and friendly home life does something else. It boosts your efforts to help your children develop a solid sense of who they are. This is what we call self-esteem.

Helping Children Build Self-Esteem

As a starting point, establishing a loving and affectionate relationship with a child is vital. However, as we are frequently told, love is not enough. We have to provide other things. A sense of positive self-esteem is also critical to our children's development and, I believe, a major factor in success. When young people like themselves, they are more likely to work harder and achieve more.

In working with delinquents and troubled young people, I realized a long time ago that the one—perhaps the only—characteristic that typified all kids who were on the wrong track in life was a poor self-image and a strong belief that they had little to offer the world. This led me to conclude that the only thing that differentiates young people who were delinquents, drug or alcohol abusers, school dropouts, school truants, or pregnant teens from their better-adjusted peers was low self-esteem.

As many psychotherapists and counselors have discovered, whenever they succeed in their work with a troubled teenager, it is usually because the therapist likes the teenager and has helped the teenager to find something good within himself or herself. As a working philosophy, I operate on the principle that within every child or adolescent who is giving parents or other adults fits is a gemstone that no one else has discovered. Helping young people discover their own talents, abilities, resources, and personal best beneath the sometimes very rough and often unappealing exterior is the trick.

For parents that is a vital task. It may be hard for those who feel let down and disappointed by a child to focus on what is truly important and valuable in the young person. I know as a parent how easy it is to focus attention on the socks left on the floor, the unmade bed, the dishes only partly washed, the homework sloppily completed, the friends who seem to be bad influences, or the failing grade in history.

More important, however, are your child's good qualities, assets, and strengths. The more a child hears about those assets, rather than being constantly reminded of shortcomings, the more likely the child will come to believe in himself or herself. When kids believe in themselves, their own worth, and their ability to make a difference in the world, then they will behave in ways that lead to their success.

How Behavior Problems Develop

In previous chapters, we discussed the factors that bring about behavior difficulties in children and adolescents. Although I'm not going to review all that information, I do want to remind you that many children with problem behaviors have difficult temperaments, and their parents have unrealistic or unreasonable expectations of them.

One other thing is necessary, as I noted at the end of Chapter 2 ("Why Do Children Develop Behavior Problems?"). Parents have to pay considerable attention to the unwanted, inappropriate, and undesired behavior for it to continue. That brings us back to criticism. Why do parents have such a difficult time seeing the good and the positive in their children?

There may be several reasons for this. But two of the most prominent reasons are that 1) there is something out of line with parents' expectations, or 2) their child is difficult to handle. In the first case, their expectations are either unrealistic or shaded by their concern about being seen as "good" parents. In the second, they have a child who has had a difficult temperament and whose behavior has been hard to manage for many years.

For example, Ronald and Jean Morgan were eager to attend their first parent-training class. In the first meeting of the 8-week program they explained to the other parents that their biggest concern was their nine-year-old son, Kurt. In their initial comments the other parents could see how upset and negative they were about Kurt.

"He's a real stinker," Ronald Morgan said.

"He's a defiant kid who throws temper tantrums and is always angry," Jean Morgan added.

Both parents had a long list of grievances about Kurt. And Kurt knew this very well. Jean had been told by his teacher during a school conference that Kurt said he felt like a "hand-me-down kid." That means, his teacher discovered, that "I'm the kid who has everything handed down to me from my older brother." That included his parents' expectations of what they wanted from their children.

Kurt wasn't at all what they expected or wanted. He was an intense, argumentative, and stubborn child; not at all like his older brother Gary, who was viewed as gifted, talented, and even brilliant.

It was relatively easy for Ronald and Jean to find fault with Kurt and to pick on what they didn't like. Kurt certainly never let them down; he was always doing something wrong to annoy or provoke them.

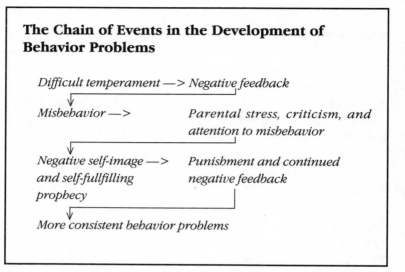

The Chain of Events in the Development of Behavior Problems

Difficult temperament —> Negative feedback

Misbehavior —>   *Parental stress, criticism, and attention to misbehavior*

Negative self-image —>   *Punishment and continued and self-fullfilling*   *negative feedback prophecy*

More consistent behavior problems

Another parent present during the opening session of this new group was Rita Carmichael. It was plain to all of us how angry she was with her thirteen-year-old daughter, Amber. In first describing her daughter to everyone that night, Rita began with, "She's thirteen and a shithead."

The forcefulness of her anger quieted everyone as Rita continued to tick off all the things that bugged her about Amber: "She doesn't do what she's supposed to. She lies, steals from me, and has terrible temper tantrums. She gets in trouble at school, and I think she uses drugs."

Judi Perna, an outgoing mother sitting across from Rita, asked her what she liked about Amber. Rita caught her breath and hesitated. "Well," she began, "I don't know. She's good at fixing things that break, but I can't think of anything else right off."

It was very clear in both the Morgan and Carmichael families that the parents' attempts at talking or communicating with their children ended in arguments. Ronald, Jean, and Rita were frequently critical of their children. Therefore, communication, reasoning, and other forms of discipline were thwarted before they began.

The Role of Criticism in the Development of More Serious Behavior Difficulties

How the communication got to be that way is less important than changing it. But for some parents it is useful to understand the evolution of this kind of negative and critical communication pattern.

Parents seldom start out being critical, blaming, or negative. Actually, most of us are very good at being positive and supportive with our children when they are infants and young toddlers.

Sometime after that (although frequently, very difficult children and stressed parents have problems as early as infancy), the child's behavior proves to be a management problem for the parents. While they may not cause a behavior problem, the parents' response after it occurs considerably affects whether that misbehavior continues and whether it gets better or worse over time. How the child responds in turn affects the future responses from parents.

In other words, the way a parent initially handles misbehavior will have either a positive or negative influence on the future of the unwanted behavior as well as on the child's reactions to the parent's discipline.

Criticism is a way of placing the spotlight on the behavior we want to eliminate. When we do that, we twist the whole concept of positive discipline into a negative. It is usually true that children aren't looking for "negative attention," but when they start to get scoldings, criticism, and their parents' devoted attention to the undesirable behavior, something strange happens: The behavior continues and sometimes gets worse.

The Mistakes Parents Make in Applying "Discipline"

When parents criticize a child, the child's self-esteem gradually erodes. If criticism and other negative ways of dealing with situations (such as belittling and shouting) continue unabated over years, a child may develop precious little sense that he or she is a good and worthwhile person.

Let me give an example of how this begins to work early in life.

Three-and-a-half-year-old Terrance is a normal little boy, and as a typical child he tries out various behaviors. One day, soon after his mother brings home a little puppy, Terrance is busily playing with the dog. Terrance starts off gently, but later becomes rougher, at one point trying to ride the puppy like a pony.

"Terrance, stop that this minute!" his mother says as she notices how the boy is treating the puppy. "Don't do that. That hurts him. How would you like it if you were a little dog and a boy did that to you? Now don't you treat him mean again."

Not more than five minutes later, Terrance is cuffing the dog on the ears, and the puppy yelps. Again his mother intervenes. "Terrance, stop being mean. That's mean what you're doing. That's not nice." As she delivers the final words, she slaps Terrance on the legs. It is Terrance's turn to let out a yelp, and he gives his mother a steely stare.

Terrance had no intention of being mean or of hurting the puppy. He didn't know any better about how to play with a small pet. But his mother's way of dealing with it was to criticize Terrance's behavior and intentions. Instead of teaching the youngster what she expected or how to play with a pet more appropriately, she harshly taught him the wrong way by emphasizing how "mean" he was and reinforcing her criticism with a slap. At the same time, she was teaching him how he could get her attention.

If similar situations happen again and again, Terrance will get the idea that he is a "bad boy." He will know very well how to upset his mother (and perhaps all adults), and he will come to believe that he is "mean." It may happen, after being told he is mean, bad, or a troublemaker a few thousand times, that he has to act that way because he believes that is his role, his fate, or his lot in life.

If Terrance engages in other misbehavior (by running in the street, playing with the fish in the fish tank, throwing temper tantrums, or hitting other children in day-care), his mother and other adults will likely feel that they have to intensify their negative and critical reactions to him to attempt to get him to be "good" and to behave. When children receive hundreds and thousands of negative messages from parents, relatives, neighbors, and teachers, they start to believe and live the messages. It is therefore important to be very much aware of how often you are using negative and critical messages with your children.

How many times do you say:

"How can you be so dumb?"
"When are you going to start listening to me?"
"Grow up and accept responsibility."
"Stop acting like a baby."
"You never listen."
"You're lazy."
"You're not trying."
"You don't care if you don't get better."
"If you're not going to even try, then don't expect me to help you."
"You're lying!"

If you're using such critical comments more than just once in a while, there's a problem.

The problem is that kids come to expect negative and critical remarks, and those remarks may reinforce the very behavior parents thought they were trying to change. The alternatives include giving attention and praise to the behavior you like, avoiding comments about undesirable behavior, and demonstrating (and praising after the child has tried your way) correct behavior.

One thing that happens in families where the parents focus on misbehavior and mistakes is that kids feel discouraged. They know very well when they mess up or make mistakes. They don't need their parents rubbing it in.

From the parents' point of view, though, they feel as if they just can't let mistakes or errors slip by without "doing something." The something they do could well be one of those "traditional" methods of dealing with children. If their child makes a mistake or misbehaves, parents who are steeped in the traditional methods of raising children think the error or misbehavior must be brought to the child's attention so it can be corrected. To do otherwise would be unthinkable to such parents.

George Anderson, known to baseball fans as Sparky Anderson, the affable and genial manager of the Detroit Tigers, has learned that pointing out mistakes is not the best way to manage baseball players. Although I don't know about his abilities as a parent, as a skipper for both the Cincinnati Reds and the Tigers he has managed his teams to more than two thousand victories. He said something in a radio interview before a Detroit Tigers' ball game in April 1991 that struck me as wisdom parents could apply.

It concerned Rob Deer, the Tigers' new right fielder who had been acquired from the Milwaukee Brewers before the start of the 1991 season.

As the season began and moved along through the month of April, Deer was mired in a terrible slump. It was late April, and Deer was hitting something like .036. In the interview, the announcer asked Sparky Anderson about Deer and his slump.

"I was just talking to Rob about that," Anderson said. "I said to him, 'I've figured it out and I want you to do me a favor. Go oh-for-four today, because if you do your batting average will drop to .028. You're twenty-nine years old, and this will be the only time in your career that you will be batting less than your age. We'll make a sign and put your batting average and your age on it and we'll take a picture. This will be great. You can always have it and you'll be able to show it to your grandchildren someday.'"

Sparky Anderson went on to say in the interview that baseball players don't need a manager when they're hitting .350 or .375. They need a manager when they're in a slump. But they don't need to be told how badly they're doing, nor do they need to be threatened with being benched.

Hearing this interview before the game and before I went to do a parent group that night, I thought there was some good advice for parents. But I was also curious to know what effect it would have on Rob Deer. I couldn't wait to get home that night and tune into the sports channel to catch the baseball scores and highlights.

Rob Deer didn't go oh-for-four that night. In fact, he went three-for-four, including a triple and home run. Over the next few weeks he went on a tear, leading the team in both home runs and RBIs.

Sparky's approach worked. If he had criticized Deer, reminding him of how much the Tigers were paying him, pointing out what he was doing wrong each time he went up to bat, and letting him know how lazy, unmotivated, unskilled, or how disappointing he was, Deer would have felt increased pressure.

"They need," Anderson said, "someone to pat them on the back and let them know that things are going to be all right."

When parents can accept their children, give them encouragement, and focus on what will help them feel good about themselves, kids have a chance to improve and to break out of their own "slumps."

The eighteenth-century French moralist Joseph Joubert summed up what I think about criticism: "Children need models more than they need critics."

Summary

There are 12 key characteristics that make for effective parenting:

- **Providing love, affection, and concern**
- **Helping children build self-esteem**
- **Having respect for children**
- **Accepting children and showing approval**
- **Having a good understanding of discipline techniques**
- **Providing clear and reasonable expectations**
- **Being consistent in handling children**
- **Setting strict and firm limits**

- Having consistent parenting approaches among all the child-care figures in the home
- Enforcing limits
- Allowing dissent and expression of feelings within the limits
- Being able to let go of our children

The child's single most important tool for successfully facing the problems, issues, and crises that arise in day-to-day life is self-esteem. Self-esteem and self-image are the key factors in how your child learns, achieves, gets along with peers, and loves others. Criticism and negative comments to children and adolescents erode self-esteem and undermine the confidence children have in themselves. These remarks also focus parental attention on the misbehavior and inappropriate behavior of young people. Such parental tactics lead to more discouraged, less competent children whose inappropriate and undesired behavior may increase.

Homework Assignment for Week 1

I. Monitor how often you use critical remarks and negative statements with your children. Do not try to do it less; just find out how often you are being critical. You may surprise yourself and discover that you criticize more than you thought. Or you could find out that you're pretty good at avoiding the negative and the critical remark. One clue that helps: We're usually most critical when we're very angry with a child.

This week watch for excessive anger and disappointment and keep a running tally of the number of critical and negative remarks you make to your child. Make a check in the space for each day for every critical comment or remark you use:

MONDAY: ————————————————————————

TUESDAY: ————————————————————————

WEDNESDAY: —————————————————————

THURSDAY: —————————————————————

FRIDAY: —————————————————————

SATURDAY: —————————————————————

SUNDAY: —————————————————————

II. The second part of the assignment is even easier. Make a list of 10 things you like and appreciate about your child (or children). That is, what are the child's strengths, assets, good qualities, positive traits, and aspects of appearance, personality, or temperament that are likely to help rather than hinder him or her in life? Write those 10 things in the space provided here.

1. —————————————————————
2. —————————————————————
3. —————————————————————
4. —————————————————————
5. —————————————————————
6. —————————————————————
7. —————————————————————
8. —————————————————————
9. —————————————————————
10. —————————————————————

5.

Week 2: Learning to Give

Praise and Attention

The second week is an exciting time for the class. Parents always come to the second session of my parenting course with greater insight into their own behavior.

"I didn't realize how often I was criticizing," said Rita Carmichael, summing up what many parents say after tracking their negative and critical remarks for a week.

And then there are the confessions:

"I really blew it this week," said Gail Hackett, the mother of three children, including an acting-out teenager. "I got so angry with him about going to school, I started yelling at him and ended up slapping him twice. I'm beginning to realize how bad my parenting skills are."

Mary Cole, the mother of twelve- and fourteen-year-old boys, came to the second session with her homework completed but with doubts about her actions. "I didn't have that many check marks in the criticism section," she readily announced to the group, "but I had some. I don't know about anyone else, but I'm not always sure what is criticism and what isn't." As she said this, Mary looked around anxiously to see if others felt the same confusion she did. Several heads nodded in agreement.

Mary went on to give an example of something that happened recently in her home. "My son Jason asked if he could go to a friend's house. It was almost dark, and he didn't have his homework done, so

I told him no. That really set him off. He started yelling at me and said, 'I hate you, you bitch! You never let me do anything.'

"I got mad myself," continued Mary. "Who wouldn't when your kid calls you a bitch? I told him he was acting immature and asked him how could he expect me to let him do anything responsible when he's acting like a little irresponsible child.

"He went stomping off to his room and slammed the door. I could hear things being thrown around the room."

A little while later, Jason came out of his room. He was calmer and asked in a nice way if he could "please" go to his friend's house. Mary almost relented but still said no.

"But what I want to know," Mary said, directing the question to the whole group, "is was that criticism when I told him he was acting immature? Wasn't he being immature and acting like a little kid? Didn't I have a right to tell him that?"

The question was a good one, and it certainly raises an important issue: When is telling the truth criticism and when is it giving our kids important feedback about their behavior?

Criticism, according to my *Webster's*, is the "art of judging merit." It also means censure and unfavorable comments either verbally or in writing. Telling a child she is immature is certainly censure and is an unfavorable comment. Does she merit this at the time? Probably. Does it help her to gain control over her behavior and to feel better about herself? The odds are it doesn't. In Mary's situation, it actually resulted in her son stomping off to his room and slamming the door.

The question, then, is whether criticism is any negative comment or censuring remark that draws attention to a perceived failing, shortcoming, inadequacy, or defect in a child. Telling a child or adolescent that she is immature, irresponsible, or acting like a younger child is definitely a critical remark. But the more important and underlying question is: Can we enhance a child or adolescent's feelings about herself and help her to gain new knowledge, self-esteem, or self-control through such criticism?

Mary's comments to her son did not accomplish any of these ends. But could Mary have handled the situation differently

---

Changing Critical Communication Into Noncritical Comments

Critical Statement: *"You're so stupid! Can't you do anything right?"*

Noncritical Statement: *"You seem to be having a tough time remembering the material you study for tests."*

Critical Statement: *"Pay attention! No wonder you don't know anything—you never listen."*

Noncritical Statement: *"It's hard for you to pay attention right now. Let's say we take a break and try again."*

Critical Statement: *"Shut up! You're not making any sense—as usual."*

Noncritical Statement: *"Can we go over this again? I don't think I follow what you're saying."*

Critical Statement: *"I don't know why you're so lazy. You're just not putting forth any effort. How do you expect to make anything of yourself if you don't try?"*

Noncritical Statement: *"Based on my conversation with you and your teacher, motivation seems to be a big problem for you. What do you think?"*

---

so she could have accomplished one of these goals? I think she could have while avoiding directing censure to her son.

One of the things that happens with kids when we focus on the unfavorable ("You're being immature") is that we may reinforce a behavior we really don't like (blowing his stack and name-calling when he is told no). Mary could have struck a blow for something she did want (maturity, self-control) by making sure she was supporting that kind of behavior. She might have done this in the very beginning by saying no in a different way. For instance, she might have said, "I'm going to say no today, but if you ask me tomorrow early enough in the evening and after your work is done I'll say yes." Or by asking him not to get angry and adding: "I expect you to handle my decisions in a mature way."

Another way of handling this would have been to withhold comment on his "immature" behavior and wait until he is acting maturely, and at that time give him positive feedback. In the scenario Mary described, if she had waited a while longer—say, until after he had blown off some steam—then she could have commented on how quickly he got over his anger ("I noticed that you got yourself back in control in record time after I told you no. I'm really proud of you.").

Reinforce Desired Behavior When It Happens by Giving Praise and Attention

While we don't always get the behavior we want, we should do something to reinforce it when it does occur. One thing we can do is employ the strategy of Giving Praise and Attention, a valuable discipline technique.

As I'm suggesting with this example of Mary's problem with an angry son, Giving Praise and Attention for the behavior we want to encourage can be substituted for criticizing behavior we don't want.

It sounds simple, but it isn't always so easy to put into practice—particularly if you're a parent who frequently criticizes. After doing the homework assignment for Week 1 ("The 12 Keys to Effective Parenting"), you should have a better idea how often you're being critical with your youngster.

Charting your behavior allows you to become more aware of how many times you make a critical, censuring comment and to cut down the frequency of such remarks.

The second part of the first week's assignment was to list the ten things you like best about your child. This list comes easily to some parents and not to others. It is especially hard for parents of an acting-out teenager or a child of any age who is out of control.

"If I don't find anything positive in my child," said Pete Hernandez, a father who was upset by the assignment, "you're implying that it's my fault. But I tell you, my thirteen-year-old never does anything I like."

Rita Carmichael couldn't wait to agree: "Amber never does anything worth praising."

Mary Cole joined in, too, stating, "It's hard to think of ten things I like. It's a lot easier to identify things I don't like than things I do."

This exercise helps parents to understand where they're focusing their attention when it comes to their kids. As Judi Perna, mother of three, said: "This exercise made me recognize some of the good things about my children that I'd been overlooking lately." Which is, of course, the point. It is designed to begin changing the focus back to what is positive, valuable, and good about our kids.

A Sampling of Positive Traits to Look for in Your Child

Personality Traits and Characteristics
Persistence
Single-mindedness
Friendliness
Humor
Optimism
Honesty
Curiosity

School and Work Habits
Dedication
Organized
Persistence
Neatness
Creativity

A Sampling of Positive Traits to Look for in Your Child (cont.)

Interests and Hobbies

Diverse interests
Productive use of time alone
Healthy Competitiveness
Constructive hobbies
Athletic skills

Peer Relationships

Plays well with friends
Is willing to share
Is considerate
Makes new friends easily
Is polite
Is compassionate

Home and Family Behavior

Is obedient
Completes chores
Is respectful
Maintains orderly habits

It was a struggle for Pete Hernandez, but he came up with five things to like about his daughter Valerie. Pete told the group she was:

1. artistic
2. smart
3. imaginative
4. willing to try new things
5. spirited

Ron and Jean Morgan, who complained about nine-year-old Kurt's temper outbursts, wrote that they liked his:

1. sense of humor
2. ability to think things through
3. artistic abilities
4. musical talents
5. physical skill at sports

Rita Carmichael, with coaxing questions and comments from other parents, admitted that Amber had these characteristics:
1. caring for others
2. sensitivity
3. ability to work hard
4. single-mindedness
5. slender physique

While these three parents each found a different set of things they liked, they typify what many parents decide are the positive traits of their children. As difficult as it may be at first, completing the exercise helps you to concentrate on what is truly important. This naturally helps you to give praise and attention to the positive behavior rather than focus on actions that are more negative and ultimately less important.

The purpose of giving praise and attention is to increase the frequency of the behavior we like in our children and to strengthen how our children feel about themselves.

Giving Attention by Describing Behavior

A behavior is reinforced when we pay attention to it. Parents can pay attention verbally simply by describing a behavior. By simply commenting, "You spent a whole hour on your math homework," you are paying attention to a behavior. The youngster knows you notice how much time (and perhaps effort) she put into her math assignment, and it's implied that you're pleased. When children receive recognition (even if no praise is involved), they are very likely to repeat that behavior in order to gain more recognition.

The best examples of this attentiveness happen when we witness the tremendous progress an infant makes almost every day during the first couple of years. What contributes to that rapid progress, development, and new learning? In part it has to do with the time and attention we devote to a child. We usually find everything about our first child wonderful, fascinating, and captivating. Every new movement, vocal sound, and skill is like a miracle. Most of us overjoyed parents are endlessly fascinated by each and every new thing. We talk about it, make videotapes, call our parents, and tell our friends about each new event.

Our children hear our comments, flattery, compliments, and prideful remarks. "Look at her crawl." "Did you see that? He almost stood up." "Isn't she pretty?" "He ate all of his carrots today." "What a strong girl." "You enjoy the water when you take a bath." "You can do it. Walk to Daddy. Look, he's walking." In such a hothouse atmosphere, young children can't fail to thrive. With their behavior the source of commentary and praise, they are at the center of a lot of positive attention. As a result, children learn quickly and feel very proud of their accomplishments. Yet a great deal of what parents do at this early age is simply to describe children's behavior aloud.

By letting kids know we notice their actions, we encourage them to repeat the same actions.

Here are some examples of descriptive remarks parents in my program have used:

"You handed me the hammer I needed."

"You made me a gift at school."

"You put away all your crayons."

"Hey, you put on your clothes all by yourself."

"Cody and Jan are playing a fun game together."

"You finished all of your breakfast."

"You remembered to wash your face."

"You straightened up the apartment all by yourself."

"You kids remembered to put your dirty clothes in the laundry basket."

It is valuable to understand how to use the technique of giving attention through descriptive remarks, because it forms the basis for giving praise in the best possible ways. Making descriptive remarks simply means commenting on behaviors and actions of your children objectively and accurately. As you become better at this, you can add a more elaborate description and more interesting words.

For instance, instead of just saying, "You made me a gift," you could say: "You made a plaster ashtray for me at school." Or, you could dress up "You put on your clothes today" by saying instead: "You picked out your own clothes all by yourself and you have on your lovely blue slacks and that neat green blouse, and you did all this while I was getting ready for work."

In other words, the more life you give to your remarks by using descriptive detail, the more likely kids are going to listen to you and realize that you're really serious about noticing their accomplishments and efforts.

When letting your daughter know that you are aware she straightened up the apartment before you got home from work, you could say: "You put away the Sunday newspapers, vacuumed the carpet, and even arranged the books on the shelf more neatly."

Such an observation leaves little doubt that you noticed exactly what she did and know it took some special effort or accomplishment on her part.

Adding Praise to Descriptive Remarks

After practicing the use of descriptive remarks that are specific and detailed, you will be ready to add praise. Both attention and praise are discipline techniques that strengthen and increase desired and appropriate behaviors. Learning to use them comfortably involves a sequence of events that goes like this:

1. Notice behavior you like.
2. Describe the behavior in an accurate and interesting way.
3. Add words of praise to your description.

Adding praise is quite simple: Just add a compliment or an encouraging comment to the descriptive remark. Here are some examples of parents' use of praise from my groups:

"I really appreciate your kindness in reading to those younger children."

"Thanks so much for your thoughtfulness in remembering to put your dirty clothes in the laundry basket."

"Good going, Jamie, you tied your shoes so neatly and you did it by yourself."

"That's wonderful. You finished your lunch and put away your dishes. I like that."

"I'm so proud of you for sticking with your English assignment and getting it finished and typed. That took concentration."

"I'm so pleased with you for deciding to go to work when you were tired and didn't feel like it. That's the mark of a hard worker."

"Zach, it's so pleasant when you play a board game with us. I enjoy your humor."

"Connie, you were such a big help when you cut the veggies for dinner. They look marvelous the way you arranged them on the plate."

"I don't know how you can be so clever! This is a very imaginative story you wrote for your English class. This deserves a high mark."

"Mark, you act so grown up when you ask me only once and then wait for my answer. I can't wait to share this good news with your father. He'll be proud, too."

More Guidelines for Giving Praise and Attention

From the discussion thus far, you probably already have a fair idea of some of the ways that these discipline techniques are used most effectively.

- Praise works best when it closely follows behaviors and actions you would like to see encouraged and strengthened. The sooner it follows the desired behavior, the better.

- Give praise only when children are behaving—not when they are misbehaving.
- As indicated, praise is best given when it is both descriptive and specific. You should not say: "You're such a fine boy." Instead be specific: "It's terrific the way you took charge and organized your group to get that project done in your class."
- Praise as many different aspects of your child's behavior as you can. Try to compliment such things as cooperativeness, compliance, use of intelligence and judgment, social skills, expressiveness, and willingness to help. Praise not only accomplishments but also efforts.
- Don't underestimate the power of adding some physical affection like a big cuddle or a kiss.

Dr. Carol E. Franz, a professor of psychology at Boston University, conducted a long-term study that showed how important physical gestures and affection are to kids as they are growing up. Following individuals from age five to age forty-one, she found that parents who were rated as warm and physically affectionate—that is, parents who held, kissed, hugged, and cuddled their children a lot—raised children who appeared to have high self-esteem and good emotional and psychological adjustment. These children grew up to be adults who were most able to have long and relatively happy marriages, raise children, develop close friendships, and engage in outside interests.

When Giving Praise and Attention, add some physical affection if that suits your child and if it is appropriate given the developmental level of your child.

- Feel free to praise your child in writing. A note of appreciation is a permanent record of your approval that can mean a lot to a child. Kids particularly enjoy notes that are a surprise and often keep and treasure them.
- Although it has only been implied so far, I would like to make it clear that effective praise does not include any criticism or negative remarks.

Many parents have trouble with this, particularly those parents who feel very discouraged by the behavior of their children and frequently find fault with them or point out their failings. Such parents will follow praise with censure in this way: "I appreciate it that you answered the telephone for Mom, but next time remember to write down the message." Or they will add criticism to praise by pointing out how a child falls short of the mark: "It was so helpful of you to do the dishes, but you never wipe off the counter top."

A word to the wise parent: Don't dilute your praise with criticism. Keep praise and attention pure. Save your criticism and your need to point out where a child has fallen short for some other occasion.

How to Counter Other Negative Influences in a Child's Life

Another aspect of giving praise and attention deserves consideration at this point. Usually at least one parent in every group will bring it up during Week 2. It can be illustrated by the following story.

Judi Perna was remarried but coming alone to the parent class. The mother of two boys and a girl, she was concerned about her older son, fourteen-year-old Nick, who had been in the most trouble—much of it for skipping school classes and not completing schoolwork. Judi told the group about a recent report card Nick received. She had praised Nick for bringing up his previously failing grades to two Cs and a C-minus.

"I'm really proud of how hard you worked to bring your grades up, Nick," Judi said to him when he showed her his report card. Nick beamed at this praise. Nick was proud of himself, and his chin seemed to be a bit higher than usual. Both Nick and his mother basked in the glow of the payoff in higher grades for his greater efforts to study and stay in school.

A little while later, when Judi was finishing putting some dishes away in the kitchen after dinner, Nick dragged in with his chin buried in his chest.

"What's wrong?" Judi asked, surprised to see the dejected look.

"It's Dad," replied Nick. "I called to tell him about my report card, and he said as far as he was concerned, a C grade was the same as an F. He said it was no big deal to get Cs. Anybody who was stupid could get Cs."

"You're not stupid," said Judi, rushing to the defense of Nick and his fragile ego. "You know you're smart. A stupid person couldn't raise his grades to C."

"I am too stupid," said Nick as he shuffled out of the kitchen. "Dad says so."

In the group, Judi was beside herself. "How can I raise his self-esteem and help him see his strengths and assets," she asked, "when his father is undoing all the good I try to do?"

Lots of parents, either single or married (and even parents who are battling the criticism and negative comments of their child's teacher), are in this position. They may be sold on giving praise and attention, but they begin to feel that their efforts are hopeless or doomed because of another parent or influential adult in the youngster's life who is essentially critical. Is there a way to overcome this?

It is important to recognize both the power and the shortcomings of using praise and attention as discipline techniques. They are powerful in that one person in a child's or adolescent's life can be influential in turning that child's or adolescent's life around. Almost all successful people I have ever met can cite one person in their life who recognized and appreciated their worth long before anyone else. Having one person who gives a child positive feedback about his or her strengths and abilities can make a difference.

Although giving praise and attention can be very powerful, it won't make up for all the negative things that happen in a youngster's life. If you are helping a child battle against great odds, then make sure you use praise and attention well. Follow the guidelines as given so far. Be sure you are descriptive and specific. Don't give in to the temptation to go overboard to compensate for other negative influences. It may be very tempting to say, "You're a great kid, Nick, and don't you ever forget it." However, Nick is likely to buy it more if you say, "Nick, it took a lot of willpower, effort, and determination on your part to begin going to school every day and spending an hour each day on your schoolwork. I am very proud of you."

Don't be phony and overly generous in praise. Also, don't try to use praise to argue a kid out of feeling bad or discouraged ("You aren't stupid, Nick. You're highly intelligent"). But let a discouraged child like Nick know what his unique strengths and assets are so he can see himself in a more objective and accurate way. One of the things we can do for kids is to let them know enough about themselves so that they can balance the negative and the critical with the real and the objective. Ultimately, you would like your child to be able to think: "Dad may say I'm stupid, but I know that I worked hard to get those grades up to Cs. And I also know that I'm a persistent guy. When I set my mind to something, I can do it. I decided to go to school every day and improve my grades and I did."

If a child succeeds in taking the criticism from another adult, weighing it for its objective validity, and then putting it in much better perspective, it becomes a perfect opportunity for you to say: "Hey, I'm really proud of you. You found some things you like about yourself and you aren't letting your dad's comments get you down. Good going!"

Summary

You can encourage appropriate and desired behaviors of children by paying attention to those behaviors and by giving praise. You can "pay attention" to a behavior by describing it aloud in front of your child. By adding complimentary words, you can turn that attention into praise. The guidelines for using praise are:

1. **Offer praise during or immediately after a behavior or activity you would like to see your child repeat.**

2. **Give praise only when children are behaving—not when they are misbehaving.**

3. **Make all praise descriptive and specific.**

4. **Praise as many different aspects of your child's behavior as you can. Try to compliment such things as cooperativeness, compliance, use of intelligence and judgment, social skills, expressiveness, and willingness to help.**

5. **Praise and honor efforts as well as accomplishments.**

6. **Add physical affection to your praise and attention when possible and when appropriate.**

7. **Feel free to praise your child in writing.**

8. **Make sure there is no hint of criticism in your words of praise.**

9. **Use praise in sincere and genuine ways.**

Homework Assignment for Week 2

Your assignment for this week is to give your child praise and attention at least five times every day. Look for the things that you like and appreciate. Concentrate on behaviors you would like to see strengthened, and be sure to give praise and attention in response to those behaviors.

Here's a tip that should help you: Pick one or more behaviors you would like to see happening more often. Frame them in positive terms. That is, make sure they are "do" actions ("I'd like my son to put his dirty clothes in the laundry basket") rather than "don't" behaviors ("I'd like him to stop leaving soiled clothes all over the bathroom floor"). Each time the positive, reframed behavior takes place, it's an opportunity to give praise and attention. If it doesn't take place, wait until it does or ask that it happen ("It would be helpful if you could pick up all your dirty clothes and put them in the laundry basket").

Select a behavior you would like to strengthen through praise and attention and write it here: ——————————————

_____
_____
_____
_____

Make sure this behavior is written in a form that makes it possible to praise (Examples: Coming into the house when I call; being on time for dinner; getting ready for bed the first time I ask; completing homework assignments; limiting phone calls to fifteen minutes; starting chores before I ask).

Make a check mark each time you use praise during this week, whether it's for the one or two behaviors you especially want to strengthen or for others. Remember: Your assignment is to use praise and attention at least five times a day. That is your goal. When the behavior you would like to strengthen isn't happening, find other behaviors to praise.

MONDAY: ——————————————————
TUESDAY: ——————————————————
WEDNESDAY: —————————————————
THURSDAY: ——————————————————
FRIDAY:———————————————————
SATURDAY: ——————————————————
SUNDAY: ————————————————————

Write in the space that follows two examples of your use of praise. Make sure that your praise follows all the guidelines listed in the Summary.

Example of Praise #1:————————————————

_____
_____
_____
_____
_____
_____
_____

Example of Praise #2: _____

_____

_____

_____

_____

_____

_____

_____

_____

6.

Week 3: Using Rewards and Privileges to Strengthen Behavior

When I walked into the meeting room for the third session of the parent-training group, almost everyone was already present. Seated around the conference table, parents were talking animatedly about their children.

Gail Hackett, the teacher and mother of three who always seemed to be excited, was telling those nearest her how she had begun making changes in her use of praise. She mentioned that Pete Hernandez had given her some useful advice as they walked together to the parking lot after last week's meeting. "He told me to relax or I was going to have a stroke," she said.

"I sure did," Pete said as he walked in the room and hung up his coat. "She gets too worked up about things with her kids."

"But I did well this week," Gail said brightly. Looking at me, she added, "I really did my homework this week—you'll be proud of me."

"Let's hear about it," I said. "It's always great to start with some success stories."

"It didn't feel natural at first," Gail began. "I felt like I was forcing it when I gave compliments to my kids."

"But you kept trying, right?" said Judi Perna.

"I sure did," agreed Gail.

And it was a good thing, too. The day before the third session, she arrived home after a tough day at school to find that her three children had tried to do something nice for her. They tried to fill her new water bed with water. But the bed hadn't been set up properly, and when she walked in there was water from one end of the apartment to the other. To let us know how serious this was, Gail added, "I have hardwood floors throughout the apartment."

Gail said she could have cried or exploded in anger with her kids. Instead, she bit her tongue and forced herself to offer praise and encouragement.

"I really appreciate your efforts to help me out, kids," she heard herself saying to them. "You're so thoughtful." Inside she was saying: "But, dammit, I have three hours of work ahead of me before I get the worst of this mess cleaned up."

For Gail, this was a triumph. She did something that would help her relationship with her children. Through praise she reinforced their efforts to be contributing members of the family. And, most importantly for her, she stopped herself from adding "but . . ." at the end of her praise.

Judi, Rita, and Pete gave Gail some positive strokes by raising their coffee cups in a toast to her. Gail patted herself on the back and said, "But do you want to know what I desperately wanted to say? I mean, what I've always done is to say something like, 'I appreciate your help, but please don't *ever* touch things until I tell you it's okay.'"

The other parents in the group said that her kids' hearts were obviously in the right place in wanting to help and pointed out that when she arrived home, her children were in fact trying to mop up the mess they had created. "That's the real reason," Judi concluded, "for giving praise."

Following Gail's story, Mary Cole raised a problem she'd encountered during the past week. "I really worked on my homework," she said, "but I find that I'm too much of a perfectionist. I have trouble praising and not telling my kids that they could have done a better job." Turning to me, she asked: "How do I handle that?"

This is a common problem. To deal with it successfully requires a reminder of the 12 Keys to Effective Parenting given in Chapter 4 (Week 1). One of the keys was accepting our children and showing approval. To really accept our children we must be able to allow them the room to learn, to make mistakes, and to develop at a normal pace. They don't always have the physical skills, the coordination, the patience, or the experience to do the kind of job we'd like. This can be true whether it's making a bed, cleaning a kitchen, helping us paint their bedroom, or completing homework.

However, we can show approval for their gradual improvement even if they do make mistakes along the way. We can assist them in this process by remembering that what we are doing is "shaping" their behavior.

Shaping Behavior

Think of the way we teach children as shaping their behavior. In any endeavor, children's behavior is inevitably less than perfect and usually not up to our standards at first. But with encouragement of the less-than-perfect efforts, the behavior can improve and gradually approach what we would like.

The effort a child initially makes is more significant than the outcome. This is true whether we're working with a toddler or an adolescent. It doesn't matter so much that the two-and-a-half-year-old didn't pick up all the blocks and toy cars. That the child tried deserves praise and encouragement: "All right! You're so helpful. I like it when you help me by picking up toys."

With a teenager, the behavior you're interested in might be a more respectful manner toward his or her parents. At first you may encounter cutting comments every day. You can elicit more respectful language by using such reinforcements as rewarding for courtesy (for instance, giving permission to go out with friends when asked in a more considerate manner).

Don't expect a perfect young man or woman in a day or a week. At times the teenager will slip up and revert to the old pattern. As time goes on, however, and with consistent reinforcement ("You asked me politely to go with your friends. Because I'm so pleased with that, I'm going to say yes."), you'll notice his or her behavior gradually becoming more respectful. And this will occur in many different situations—when you ask to have the lawn raked, for instance, or when you and your daughter or son have a difference of opinion.

In the two examples above, you have shaped the behavior of the child: The toddler cheerfully picks up toys when asked and the teenager speaks to you more respectfully. That is the way shaping works: You use reinforcements like Praise and Rewards to shape your child's behavior until it is very close to what you desire.

Don't negate the effectiveness of the praise you are using by slipping back into criticism when children don't achieve the ultimate result you're looking for. Keep using praise. Gradually expect and reinforce more mature behavior. All along, though, remain realistic and understand that you are shaping future behavior.

The Technique of Giving Rewards and Privileges

The discipline technique introduced in the third week of the class is Giving Rewards and Privileges. Rewards and Privileges, like Praise and Attention, are reinforcers that help to shape our children's behavior in the way we want it.

Most kids will work for payoffs. When you reinforce certain behaviors of your children by giving rewards, privileges, opportunities, and activities, those behaviors are strengthened. Giving a specific consequence for a specific behavior helps to establish appropriate and desired behaviors and actions. Children and teenagers learn to do things that lead to payoffs or positive consequences.

It's important for parents to learn how to use the Giving of Rewards and Privileges properly as part of their repertoire of discipline skills designed to bring about new behaviors or strengthen old ones.

The general principle is very straightforward: When you follow a desired behavior with a positive consequence, the desired behavior will usually become stronger.

There are three rules to keep in mind in order to Give Rewards and Privileges effectively:

1. Be clear about what you expect and the behavior you want strengthened.
2. Choose a payoff in the form of a reward, privilege, opportunity, or activity that your child deems highly desirable.
3. Give that payoff only after the child has earned it through good and appropriate behavior.

While many parents argue that giving rewards is artificial and robs kids of incentives, the fact is that all parents use this technique in one way or another, and all children learn from it. A story Mary Cole related about her fourteen-year-old son, Jason, illustrated this point. "I used a reward in this situation," Mary said, "but I doubt that I used it correctly."

In his most appealing and winning voice, Mary told the group, Jason had asked her to buy him a new pair of gym shoes, and added: "I've just got to have them, Mom. Everyone is wearing these shoes at school."

Mary asked the cost, which Jason had not mentioned in his request.

"They're only a hundred and fifteen dollars," Jason said nonchalantly. "Actually, that's cheap because they're regularly a hundred and thirty-five dollars."

"That's an awful lot of money," said Mary.

"I know, Mom," said Jason, beginning to plead his case, "but I've just got to have them. I'll feel like a total nerd if I have to wear these old shoes."

Mary's thoughts went back to her own high school days when she frequently felt like the only one in her school who didn't wear "cool" clothes.

"Well," Mary said reluctantly, "I'll think about it."

She didn't think very long, and by the end of the next weekend Jason had his expensive gym shoes. Mary, although a hundred and fifteen dollars poorer, could take a measure of comfort in the fact that for the time being her son would not have to worry about being a nerd at school.

In the group, though, Mary wondered if she had done the right thing. By using the reward of a new pair of shoes she wasn't sure that she had actually reinforced a positive behavior.

A Payoff Reinforces the Behavior It Follows

When kids get a payoff—in this instance, the payoff was a new pair of expensive gym shoes—some behavior is reinforced. Jason Cole's behavior was to request new shoes, argue the necessity of getting them, and rekindle a painful memory in his mother. Those, then, are the behaviors most likely to be repeated. If he follows the same procedure in the future, Jason has every reason to believe there will be a similar payoff from his mother.

Sometimes parents are very anxious to provide a comfortable life for their children. They do many nice things for them without asking or demanding much in return. They may then complain that although they are always kind and generous with their children, they don't get back much for their efforts. Rita Carmichael was like this. Her thirteen-year-old daughter, Amber, expected Rita to continue to do all of the things she'd come to take for granted without giving back much in the way of desired and helpful behavior.

Amber had been arrested for shoplifting and was often hostile and uncooperative at home. Rita told the class that her daughter didn't do requested chores and was often defiant.

When Amber had returned home from a detention center, Rita told her daughter that she hoped they could get along better. "All you have to do," Rita told her daughter, "is follow the rules, do your chores, and listen to me more often."

A few days later, Rita asked Amber to clean her room. "No problem, Ma," responded Amber. She'd be glad to clean her room, she said, but at the moment she was going to Carrie's house. She promised Rita that she would clean her bedroom as soon as she got home. Instead of stopping Amber, setting limits, or placing a restriction on her, Rita allowed Amber to leave. And Rita ended up cleaning the bedroom herself. As she folded Amber's clothes and vacuumed the carpet, she found herself hoping that Amber appreciated how hard Rita worked on the room and how nice it looked. She wished that her daughter would want to keep it looking good. Did Rita's action lead to a change in Amber's behavior? Was Amber more likely to clean the room herself the next time she was asked to do so?

Certainly not. Amber always found excuses—she was too busy or too tired out from school to do her chores. Instead of coming home right after school and doing her homework and chores, she went to her girlfriend's house. She did this despite her mother's rule that Amber had to ask permission to go out in the afternoon after school.

Rita told the group that she didn't really know what else to do.

How to Use Rewards and Privileges to Get the Behavior You Want

Sometimes parents like Rita are doing everything they know how to do. However, they must use Rewards and Privileges to reinforce and strengthen more appropriate behaviors with their children. It is certainly important to Rita that Amber do her chores, obey her mother, and follow all major rules. Rita might be able to accomplish these goals by Giving Rewards and Privileges in effective ways.

One place for Rita to start would be to state her expectations: to tell Amber that she expects her room to be cleaned every day. Furthermore, she should add that Amber may go to Carrie's only after the room is clean.

After Amber cleans her room and after she asks permission

to go to her girlfriend's house, Rita should say: "Your room looks so neat and tidy. Your hard work paid off. For cleaning your room and asking me for permission, you may go to Carrie's now." Amber gets the privilege of going to her friend's house for cleaning her room and remembering to ask for permission.

Rita is not using common sense when she does nice things for Amber before her daughter earns them. Rita should remember that cleaning Amber's room may be a way of avoiding a conflict, but it gives Amber a reward she doesn't deserve. In effect, what it does is reinforce Amber's pattern of making promises about how she'll behave in the future and failing to obey her mother's request.

Never Give Rewards and Privileges Before the Desired Behavior Occurs

Rewards and privileges should be given only *after* a desired or appropriate behavior occurs. They should not be given ahead of time—as Rita did when she cleaned Amber's room for her. Every parent has had this experience at one time or another. Your kid wants to do something—let's say go to a basketball game. But he also has homework to be completed. "Let me go to the game," he tells you. "I promise I'll get my homework done as soon as I get home." Being a natural pushover as well as wanting to believe your kid's promise, you say: "Okay, but you've got to do it before you go to bed."

"No problem" is the kid's last assurance before departing for the basketball game. We know what happens next. When he arrives home (somewhat later than he or you expected), he is tired: "I'm really beat, Dad. I guess I'll do the homework in the morning. I'll set the alarm for an hour earlier and get up and do it." That doesn't quite work, and your kid trots off to school without finishing the work. Meanwhile, he got to go to the basketball game.

After this has happened a few times, the effective parent wises up and insists on results first: "Get your homework done, show it to me, and then we'll talk about the basketball game."

Don't Use Rewards to Stop Misbehavior

When I introduce the technique of Giving Rewards and Privileges in a class, I find that there is always at least one parent in the group who objects on the grounds that they are bribes. "If you use a promise of a reward to get a behavior you want," the typical parental comment goes, "that is a bribe."

I see it differently. Bribes are rewards or treats you give to stop misbehavior. They give your kid the idea that this is a way to extort money or rewards from you. Giving Rewards and Privileges to stop the behaviors you don't want actually reinforces undesired behavior. A child who is given a payoff for stopping a misbehavior will learn that if she continues to misbehave, she will receive a payoff each time she stops it. That's an incentive to keep misbehaving.

Judi Perna offered an example illustrating this point. "I know what you're talking about," she said. "We did that with my four-year-old son Jerry when my husband and I took him shopping in a department store." She went on to relate how one day she and her second husband were going shopping with Jerry and had a fairly extensive list of items to buy. When they got to the store, Jerry was told he had to sit in the cart, which Dad was going to push.

Sitting in the cart was fine with Jerry at first, but soon boredom set in, and he began to crawl out of the cart. He wriggled out of the seat and down the side of the cart while his father was comparing prices of auto rust-remover on a shelf. When his father turned around, Jerry was walking down the aisle looking for something more interesting. His father called to him and Jerry stopped, waiting for his father to push the cart to him.

"I thought I told you to stay in the cart," his father said. Jerry silently looked up at him with innocent big brown eyes.

"Back in the cart," his father said. Jerry turned to run, and his father's long arms reached out and grabbed the back of his shirt. Without saying anything more, the father lifted the boy up and tried to direct his squirming feet into the cart.

"No! No cart!" Jerry screeched. Other shoppers began to crane their necks to catch the action. That only made Jerry's father more determined to win this one. Jerry's legs stiffened as if he had a sudden case of rigor mortis. Somehow they just wouldn't go in the right holes in the cart. Jerry continued to screech and squirm. His father didn't like the idea of being shown up as inept at this parenting business and began to talk to Jerry through clenched teeth. "Get in there! You have to sit in the cart while we are shopping." Every word was emphasized as if Jerry would hear and obey better if the words were enunciated plainly. "Sit in the cart," he said.

"No. Let me down!" wailed Jerry. "I'll walk beside you."

"No," insisted his father. "In the cart and I'll give you some gum when we get to the cash register."

"Gum," said Jerry, lapsing into one-syllable sentences.

"Not now," said his father, whose own sentences weren't much more sophisticated. "When we get to the cash register."

Judi, having heard the commotion, came back from the children's clothing aisle to help out. "I've got some gum in my purse," she offered. "Sit down and I'll give you some gum," she said to Jerry while digging around in the bottom of her purse. Finding it, she quickly unwrapped a stick of chewing gum and shoved it into Jerry's mouth. Jerry sat in the cart and his dad began pushing him quickly to get away from the other customers who were watching this domestic scene.

About ten minutes later, Jerry tired of the gum and the lack of stimulation. He started to move around in the seat and said he wanted to walk now. His father looked around for Judi and asked her for more gum to use to quiet Jerry. The youngster eagerly accepted another stick of gum as it provided a few minutes of diversion from the boring shopping trip.

What Jerry was learning, if not consciously at least unconsciously, was that the way to get attention and some gum is to start to crawl out of the cart or to wail about wanting to walk. It works every time. The gum is a bribe. It was meant to quiet Jerry down and to keep him in the cart without creating a scene. All Jerry has to do is threaten a scene and the gum comes out of the purse. The parent has lost control of this technique and the kid is definitely in control. Who has trained whom?

Judi and her husband could have rescued this situation and used the reward of gum effectively with just a slight alteration in their procedure. Instead of following his screeching and threats (to get out of the cart) with the gum, they could have offered it to him when he was seated in the cart and quiet. Either Dad or Mom could have said: "When you are seated in the cart and quiet, then you get gum."

Rewards and Privileges Can Be Given Spontaneously or Through an Advance Promise

Pete Hernandez handled his daughter's request for a new pair of jeans in a different way. Thirteen-year-old Valerie had asked to have a new pair of jeans "like all the other kids are wearing." Pete told his daughter that he'd have to think about it because the jeans would cost a lot of money.

In the meantime, Valerie was asked to baby-sit for two young neighborhood children. She was excited about the opportunity to baby-sit because it was her first real chance to earn some money by working outside of home.

Nervously, Valerie walked to the end of her street to baby-sit for the first time. Before she left the house, she asked her dad and his girlfriend if she could call them on the phone if there were any problems.

Twenty-five minutes later, the first call came. "What should I do if they won't come in from outside?" Valerie asked. Kerrie, her father's girlfriend, offered a suggestion.

Two hours went by before Valerie called again. "Now they won't go to sleep," she reported. "They said they're scared. What should I do?" Again, Kerrie had a helpful idea. "Thanks, a lot," said Valerie gratefully.

When the parents of the two children came home that night, Valerie was watching TV while the children were fast asleep in their beds. The kitchen and family room were spotless. They cheerfully handed Valerie a twenty-dollar bill.

The next day Pete told Valerie that the children's mother called to say how happy they were with Valerie's baby-sitting and they asked if they could hire her again sometime.

"You know," Pete said to Valerie, "I think you did very well for your first time baby-sitting. You handled it like a veteran. That new pair of jeans you want? I think you deserve them. I'll tell you what, you put in fifteen of your twenty dollars and I'll pay the rest. What do you say?"

"That's cool," said Valerie. They made plans to go to the mall the next day.

Pete's story aptly illustrated that Giving Rewards and Privileges can be a useful way for parents to motivate kids to keep doing an approved and desirable behavior. Pete Hernandez wanted Valerie to learn the value of money and take more responsibility for earning money to pay for clothes she wanted. By helping her to buy her jeans, he reinforced these behaviors. In the future, not only is Valerie more likely to act in a responsible way when working for someone else, but she is also more likely to contribute to the cost of items she'd like to buy.

Pete didn't have to make any deals with Valerie before he said he would buy the jeans. Nor did he promise that "if you act responsibly when you baby-sit, I'll buy you new jeans." Instead, the reward came spontaneously after Valerie showed mature and responsible behavior. That's important to remember: Rewards and privileges don't have to be promised ahead of time. They can be given on the spur of the moment because you are pleased with your child's behavior.

Rewards Don't Have to Be Tangible

Many parents object to using money, other tangible items that cost money, food, or candy as a reward to bring about desirable behavior. In almost every parenting group I run, a parent will say: "I don't have a lot of money to be spending on getting my kids to do the right thing."

Spending money isn't all that important to the effective

use of this discipline technique. What is important is that you understand and utilize the key principle, which says that any behavior that is reinforced is likely to occur again, not that any behavior that is expensively or tangibly reinforced will occur again.

The important thing is to notice and reinforce the behavior you like. When your child has struggled through and completed a tough school assignment, remembered to brush her teeth, made a stab at cleaning his room, handled a difficult situation with a teacher, gone to bed without crying, or gone out of the way to do something nice for an elderly neighbor, you can increase the chances that she or he will do something similar in the future by not only giving verbal praise and attention but also adding a special reward or extra privilege.

The idea of a celebration works well with kids, too. Both young people and their parents often feel better about a celebration than they do about cash being dished out for an achievement. While cash may feel cold to both sides, there's certainly nothing cold about a genuine celebration in honor of an accomplishment or a special effort.

For instance, when fourteen-year-old John turned around a school year headed for disaster by working hard to rescue three grades that had been failures earlier in the year, his mother planned a celebration.

Keeping it a secret was part of the fun. She cooked a special meal of his favorite foods, invited his favorite aunt and uncle as well as his best buddy, and brought out the best china and candles. John was surprised, and he loved the attention. He knew everyone at the celebration dinner was pleased over what he'd accomplished at school. The royal treatment made John feel really special, and it was an extra payoff—besides his passing grades—for putting forth tremendous effort at school.

In a parent-training workshop I conducted in a church one winter, a mother in the group said that her family had a special way to carry out the idea of a celebration. "We have the tradition of the red china," she said. Curiosity aroused, other parents asked her to tell the group about red china.

"The tradition," she explained, "has to do with who gets to eat off special china. We have one place setting of red china. When someone does something really noteworthy, that person is honored by getting the red china at their place at the dinner table. That makes them feel proud and honored, and everyone else is always anxious to find out what they've done to deserve it. It makes our 'red china dinners' very special."

All of which goes to show that when families are truly happy and pleased with the accomplishments of a member, there are any

---

A Sampling of Rewards and Privileges for Children and Teens

Here are some things parents in my groups have used as rewards and privileges for their children and teens:

Stars
A trip to the playground
Popsicles
Having a book read to them
Picking the video for the family to rent
Using the family car
Dried fruit
A trip to the library to select books
An hour away with friends
A trip to the mall
Going to the ice cream shop
An afternoon at the zoo
Staying up a half hour later
Playing outside later in the evening
Extra time to watch television
Points on a chart that can be exchanged for other rewards
Roller-skating trip
Having a friend stay overnight

---

number of delightful ways to send the message that "we're proud of you, and keep up the good work."

Troubleshooting the Giving of Rewards and Privileges

While children usually like the idea of rewards and extra privileges, sometimes things go wrong with their use. For instance, a child or teen can fail to keep up his or her end of the bargain when there is a prearranged incentive program. Take this dilemma that Pete Hernandez reported with his daughter. "I told Valerie that if she could stay out of trouble for one month," Pete told a group of parents, "I'd let her take the gymnastics class she wanted."

Valerie was, Pete said, absolutely delighted with this arrangement and assured her father it would be a "piece of cake." Three days later, however, Valerie was suspended from school for swearing at a teacher. "I guess some incentives aren't going to work with Valerie," Pete concluded in frustration.

Pete's conclusion may have been premature. In fact, given the kind of incentive program he had set up, it's not clear what exactly went wrong. There are at least a couple of possibilities.

One is that Pete may have asked something of Valerie that was impossible to attain. Even though Valerie said staying out of trouble would be easy and meant it at the time, she had not gone for more than a couple of weeks all year without some kind of difficulty at school. The incentive—being enrolled in a gymnastics class—was clearly one Valerie desired. Yet asking her to do something she hadn't done before and to do it over a long period of time (in this case, one month was a long time for Valerie) was expecting too much.

It would have been more realistic to make the time period shorter (say three days to start with) and change the incentive (perhaps awarding Valerie ten points toward a total of one hundred needed to get enrolled) to make it more realistic for Valerie to achieve success.

Pete could have set this up this way: "If you do not get a suspension or a detention for three days, you will earn ten points. For every three days of school you go without a suspension or detention, you will earn an additional ten points. When you have accumulated one hundred points, you will be enrolled in the next class."

As suggested by this rewording of the contract, a second problem with Pete's original agreement was that "staying out of trouble" was too vague and unspecified. That left too many potential areas of confusion, which could lead to arguments and to Valerie eventually giving up because it was either too hard or because she was "in trouble" in a way that had not been considered in the beginning.

Build in a Way to End Rewards and Privileges

Parents must build into any prearranged incentive program a way for the system to end. We don't want kids to come to expect money or rewards every time they do something worthwhile.

Rewards and privileges are phased out by gradually withdrawing and changing the incentive program. Sometimes children ask for an end to a program, and other times it can end without either parents or children remarking about it. If it is phased out, either the system is changed in some way so that more effort or a greater accomplishment is required to earn a payoff, or the reward or privilege is no longer given every time as it was at first. If you gave a child a cookie every time he tied his shoes in the beginning, you can change that to every third time, then every fifth time, and finally, because the behavior becomes automatic, not at all.

Even as you phase out a reward or privilege, it is essential to continue to use verbal praise and attention. No matter what reward, incentive, or payoff is given, make sure that you always say how pleased and proud you are of an effort or accomplishment. In the long run, that's what we want kids to be working for—not for the new pair of expensive gym shoes.

Summary

Most all of us try to gain rewards and payoffs while avoiding pain or negative results. When a child's behavior is followed by a reinforcer, that behavior is strengthened and is likely to occur again. Through reinforcement, children and teenagers learn to do things that lead to positive consequences.

It is therefore important for parents to know how to use rewards, payoffs, and positive consequences as part of their repertoire of discipline skills. Reinforcers are especially important for helping establish new behaviors or a pattern of behavior with your children.

Three rules for the effective use of rewards and privileges are:

1. Be clear about what you expect and the behavior you want strengthened.
2. Choose a payoff in the form of a reward, privilege, opportunity, or activity that your child deems highly desirable.
3. Give that payoff only after the child has earned it through good and appropriate behavior.

Other points to keep in mind when using rewards and privileges include:

- Give rewards and privileges immediately after a desired behavior.
- Do not use the reward or privilege to stop a misbehavior.

- Use a verbal description and praise to accompany the reward or privilege.
- Sometimes be spontaneous in giving a reward or privilege; sometimes tell a child ahead of time how he or she might earn a special reward.
- Be specific in deciding the exact behavior you wish to reinforce.
- Be realistic in setting your expectation for how your child can earn the reward or payoff.

Homework Assignment for Week 3

The homework assignment for this week is to select a specific behavior of your child that you would like to see increased or strengthened.

Write that behavior here: ———————————————

———————————————————————————
———————————————————————————
———————————————————————————
———————————————————————————
———————————————————————————

To increase or strengthen that behavior, give a reward or privilege after the behavior has taken place. Write the reward, privilege, opportunity, or activity you plan to use to encourage the desired behavior written above: ———————————

———————————————————————————
———————————————————————————
———————————————————————————
———————————————————————————
———————————————————————————

Make a check mark on the lines that follow on each day that you use a reward or privilege to reinforce the behavior you have indicated above:

MONDAY: —————————————————————————

TUESDAY: —————————————————————————

WEDNESDAY: ————————————————————————

THURSDAY: —————————————————————————

FRIDAY: —————————————————————————

SATURDAY: —————————————————————————

SUNDAY: —————————————————————————

7.

Week 4: Using Reminder Praise and Increasing Compliance with Expectations

I can't believe it," Judi Perna said at the beginning of Week 4. "I'm just using praise and my kids are doing their chores."

"My son is going to school more," echoed Gail Hackett.

After three weeks of practice in using the techniques we've talked about so far, many parents begin to see results. They tell the group members the kinds of improvements they see at home.

"I'm not getting as angry at my son," said Gail Hackett, "and I certainly haven't slapped him lately. And I'm finding that I feel more positive as I say more positive things to him."

"I have to tell you this," said Pete Hernandez as he looked around the room at the other parents. "I've thought of more things I like about Valerie. She's not as bad as I used to think. We're even talking more."

As in every other session, during the fourth session of my class parents reveal a range of experiences from the past week. Those with success stories offer encouragement to others who haven't yet seen the kinds of progress they would like. But parents impatient for immediate positive feedback can become discouraged if their efforts seem to meet little reward.

"I'm trying to give praise and rewards," said Rita Carmichael, "but I still get the same behavior from Amber. When she finally did work at straightening up her room, I told her how helpful she was. Then she didn't do another chore for several days. Why should I keep being nice to her?"

Ron Morgan told the group he knew exactly what Rita was saying. "Kurt puts off doing his homework even though we give him rewards and praise when he does it immediately. It's like praise doesn't work with him."

There may be several explanations for a child's lackluster response to parents' efforts at giving praise, attention, rewards, and privileges to reinforce desired behavior. First of all, it is important to keep in mind that sometimes children refuse to change because they are waiting to see if your new ways of dealing with them will be consistent or permanent, or if they represent merely a passing phase. That is, children may recognize and like the idea of getting more praise and rewards for positive behavior but doubt that it will continue. This is often the case in families where parents have been inconsistent over the years. The children may have seen their parents attempt to change their parenting or discipline styles a number of times. If the children begin to respond to praise, they risk being disappointed when the parents revert to a more critical style.

Another common reason for lackluster results is parents setting unrealistic goals for improvement or failing to target the behavior they want to see improved. If a parent seeks generalized, undefined changes in a child's behavior ("I just want her to be good and follow the rules"), it becomes very difficult for the child to satisfy the parent's goals, since it's nearly impossible to respond well in every realm of behavior. Moreover, it's even more difficult for parents to know when improvement has occurred if criteria for improvement are so vague.

Rita may want Amber to obey all rules, address her respectfully, go to school, study hard, and clean her room. Not only is that asking a great deal (and therefore setting unrealistic expectations), but it means that Rita is likely to assess progress so generally that it will be hard for her to notice progress in any one area if other areas aren't going well. By taking one behavior at a time, Rita has a much better chance of acting positively and consistently with respect to that behavior of Amber's (say, cleaning her bedroom) and will be able to tell whether there is improvement.

Targeting specific behavior for improvement ideally should have begun with the second homework assignment, when parents began giving praise, and continued with the third one (Giving Rewards and Privileges). I want parents to begin to narrow down their concerns, to target specific behaviors to work on, and to set realistic expectations. If you don't do this, you are almost certainly setting the stage for failure rather than success.

One other possible explanation for some parents' lack of success at this point rests with their own difficulties in being consistent with the techniques we've talked about so far. Most discipline techniques, as I mentioned in Chapter 1 ("What Can Parents Accomplish in 8 Weeks?"), depend on a consistent approach by parents. If parents are praising and rewarding behavior, but doing so inconsistently and interspersing negative attention or criticism, they are sabotaging their own efforts.

Whether or not parents have seen improvement in their children's behavior, all come to the fourth session loaded with questions arising from their efforts over the past days and weeks as well as from their increased attention to their own and their children's behavior. Week 4, then, starts out by concentrating on techniques to refine ways to use Praise and Attention wisely and give Rewards and Privileges effectively.

Adding Reminder Praise to Your Repertoire of Skills

One of the common and important questions parents ask during Week 4 concerns how to praise their children's progress without inadvertently reinforcing the very problem they want to eliminate.

Gail Hackett raised this issue as we discussed the advantages of targeting behavior for improvement. Asked what behavior she wanted to work on with her son, she answered without hesitation: "I want Josh to go to school every day."

"In other words," I said, "you want him to attend more days of school than he's attending now."

"Exactly," Gail agreed.

"Now, then," I said to Gail, "you want your son to attend school more often. Let's use this as a model for other parents. What are ways of praising him and giving rewards and privileges?"

"That's obvious," said a father. "If he goes to school, you tell him: 'I really appreciate it that you went to school today. Good going.'"

"But, today, he only went the first three hours," complained Gail. "How can I praise him for that?"

"Try giving him reinforcement for what he did accomplish," I suggested.

"You mean," she said, "I could tell him I'm happy he went the first three hours."

"Why not?" said Ron Morgan, seated next to Gail.

"Won't that tell him he can get away with attending only three classes?" responded Gail.

"Not," I said, "if you let him know how pleased you are that he was able to stick it out for three class periods in a way that does not suggest you're entirely satisfied or that's all he ever has to attend to please you."

The situation Gail Hackett described calls for the discipline technique of Reminder Praise. This is a way of letting kids know what they're doing right while reminding them of the behavior they are avoiding.

Consider Gail's situation with Josh. Josh had gone to school for three of six hours. She was pleased because he'd attended three classes instead of missing the whole day. This is an opportunity to tell him so. Using Reminder Praise, she'd say something like this: "You stuck it out for three classes today instead of skipping the whole day. I'm proud of you."

The difference between Praise and Attention and Reminder Praise is in the key phrase "instead of." Reminder Praise offers a pat on the back for choosing a positive behavior over a negative one, and recognizes that choice in the compliment with such phrases as "rather than," "and not," "without," and "instead of."

Other examples of using Reminder Praise include:

"I've noticed you've treated your sister with kindness lately rather than teasing her. I like that."

"You went to your special school this morning without getting angry. That's a big improvement and I'm really proud of you."

"You did your chores without arguing with me. I'm so pleased about that."

Using Reminder Praise can be confusing for parents as they try to integrate this type of praise into their former ways of talking to their children. An incident Judi Perna recalled and told to the group illustrates this.

"My son Nick has started to go to church on Wednesday nights," she related to the other parents. "He does this when I'm at school taking a class. One of his chores is to look after his little brother. Anyway, last Wednesday he took his brother to church with him, which is fine. But just after I got home from my class, he called and asked if he could stay later because some of the guys wanted to play basketball in the church gym. I was tired and just said no.

"Well, he didn't come home and I began to worry when it got to be nine-thirty. When he finally came home about a half hour later, I was really steaming. So, should I use Reminder Praise to let him know I like him going to church but I don't like him staying late and playing basketball without my permission?"

"In a word, no," I replied.

And why not? Because in using Reminder Praise you have to have two interrelated but mutually exclusive behaviors. That is, the good behavior has to be chosen over the undesired behavior. But Judi's son didn't go to church *rather than* playing basketball without permission; going to church and taking care of his brother had nothing to do with staying late to play basketball without permission.

The use of Reminder Praise in this case might have gone something like this: "Nick, I'm excited and pleased that you're attending church and taking care of Jerry instead of shirking religion and not caring about your brother."

There are other problems, though, that require other methods of attack than Reminder Praise. She could simply praise him for attending church and being responsible in caring for his sibling. Yet the other problems—staying out late without permission and disobedience—have to be addressed. Starting out with praise ("You're doing a very good thing for yourself by attending church, and I'm pleased for you") is a way of providing encouragement and letting him know how happy you are with an aspect of his behavior. But at some point—probably best when you're under control and not too angry—the other issues have to be talked about. Addressing them in the right way is crucial.

Can You Use Praise with an Out-of-Control Kid?

Another question frequently raised in the fourth session concerns the difficult and angry child who is out of control. Parents who are used to reacting in angry ways themselves and who are now told to look for opportunities to use praise can become confused about how to use praise with the angry young person.

For example, Pat Loughman, the mother of a fifteen-year-old girl, told the group about her daughter's anxiety and agitation as she was getting ready to go to a new high school for the first time.

"It wasn't my idea to go to this dumb school," her daughter Maura said, "and all the other kids there will be snobs."

As Maura talked, she became increasingly upset. When her hair wasn't falling into place the way she liked it, she hurled her hairbrush across the room, making a mark on the wall.

"Well," said her mother, "does that little outburst make you feel better?"

That was the wrong thing to say, because it triggered off more anger as the girl's feelings spun out of control. Crying and shouting at her mother, Maura flew to her room, slammed the door, and shouted that she'd never go to school again.

Could Pat Loughman have used praise? How do you do that with an angry adolescent?

There are several issues here. One has to do with finding a way to use praise in a volatile situation. A parent obviously can't praise a child for working herself up into an angry frenzy, throwing her hairbrush across the room, or running in tears to her room.

However, if she gets over her angry outburst sooner than usual, finds a way of resolving the issue, or expresses her emotions more appropriately, you do have an opportunity to use Reminder Praise or one of the other discipline techniques we've discussed so far.

Using Praise and Attention, Pat might say: "You know what I think? You were mad but you found something positive about the school that helps you hang in there. I like that kind of thinking."

Giving Rewards and Privileges: "I know it won't be easy getting used to a brand new school. Hang in there for the rest of the year and we'll let you visit your cousin in California this summer."

Using Reminder Praise: "When you get over your angry outbursts quickly instead of letting them go on for hours, I feel you're becoming more mature."

Basic Principles for Using Reminder Praise

There are some basic principles about using Reminder Praise that ought to be stated at this point.

1. Reminder Praise works best when it is given at the time

of the behavior you would like to reinforce. It must always be constructed around a situation that shows improvement. Use it when the young person is doing something well that she hasn't always done quite as well in the past.

For instance, if Valerie Hernandez gets mad at her father's live-in partner for trying to boss her around and "be like my mom," but handles it better than usual this time, Reminder Praise can be employed. "You're really showing signs of growing up in your thinking. I appreciate it when you can find positive things about Kerrie without just looking for the ways in which she annoys you."

Another example is when Amber storms out of the house intent on running away, but returns less than an hour later. Her mother could say: "Thanks for coming back on your own and for not staying gone longer. That shows greater self-control."

2. Each time you use Reminder Praise, the praiseworthy behavior must be incompatible with the behavior that's avoided. That is, the child can't be doing both; one necessarily cancels out the other. Valerie cannot spew out undiluted hatred of her father's girlfriend while at the same time finding something good to say about her. Amber cannot run away and have to be forced to return home and also come home in a short period of time voluntarily. Gail's son Josh can't treat his mother with respect and swear at the same time. Nor can Judi's son Nick come home on time from church and be late.

Reminder Praise lets kids know that you notice what they are doing right and notifies them that you notice they aren't doing something they used to do. This technique effectively undermines a young person's contention that "you never notice when I make improvements." You do notice and you comment on it.

3. As mentioned, an essential part of using Reminder Praise effectively has to do with the connector words you put in between

the two clauses in your sentence. They should be phrases like "instead of," "without," "for not," and "rather than."

Bringing About Compliant Behavior

When we use Praise and Attention, Rewards and Privileges, or Reminder Praise, we are usually reinforcing some form of compliance behavior in our kids. The issue of compliance is important. When parents are upset with a child or adolescent, usually the problem comes down to the child "not minding" or "not listening." I find that that's one of the predominant issues when parents bring youngsters to counseling or therapy. They have a child who isn't minding. With the discipline techniques we've talked about so far—those designed to encourage desired and appropriate behaviors—you have three ways to reinforce compliant behavior. When your children do what you ask, obey commands and requests, or follow rules, you can use Praise and Attention, Rewards and Privileges, or Reminder Praise.

But there is another process that helps a great deal in this campaign to bring about more compliant behavior. It's called the 5-Step Method of Increasing Compliance. It serves as a way of letting your child know your expectations, communicating the consequences for compliance and noncompliance, and monitoring your own follow-through.

1. *Identify the problem.* In considering how to increase a child's compliance, it's important to identify his or her problem behaviors and times when he or she doesn't mind. You must be able to formulate the problem in a clear way. Examples of this are:

> *"She won't stay in her bed at night."*
> *"He constantly interrupts me when I'm on the phone."*
> *"She always lies about where she's going."*

Three Ways to Reinforce Compliant Behavior

Here are examples of the use of Praise and Attention, Rewards and Privileges, and Reminder Praise to reinforce compliance in three different situations.

Praise and Attention

"You slept in your own bed all night. That's terrific!"

"Hey, you got over your temper tantrum really quickly. I'm impressed."

"Done with your school work so soon? Nice going."

Rewards and Privileges

"When you sleep in your own bed all night, I'm really pleased. For that you get to pick the game we're going to play today."

"When your temper tantrum is over and the toys are put away, then we'll race your new car."

"You've finished all of your homework. I'm really proud of you, because I know you had several pages of math to do. Let's go to the video store and you can choose a movie for us to watch tonight."

Reminder Praise

"Good going. You slept the whole night in your own bed without waking up and coming into our bedroom."

"You handled it really well when I said we couldn't go to the game. I'm really proud of you when you say 'Okay, Mom' instead of getting mad."

"You should be as pleased as I am about the way you dealt with your school work tonight. You got right to it and got it down without putting it off and playing video games. Excellent!"

Now, having identified the problem, you must be able to state the problem in a positive way, setting up an expectation. This means that the original problem has to be converted into a behavior or expectation you have. For instance, the problems just identified can be changed into behavioral expectations:

"I would like her to go to sleep in her own bed and stay there for the whole night."

"I would like him to find something to do on his own so that he doesn't interrupt me when I'm on the phone."

"She should tell the truth more often about where she's going with her friends."

2. *Tell your child your expectation.* Having formulated the problem into a "do" behavior rather than a "don't," it's time to communicate this expectation to your child. In a very clear and authoritative way, you tell your child your expectation:

"I expect that you will go to sleep in your own bed and stay there the whole night."

"I expect that when I'm on the phone you will play with your toys until I'm finished with my conversation."

"The rule in this family is that you will always tell the truth about where you're going."

There should be no question about what you expect and what you want your youngster to do.

3. *Have the child repeat the expectation back to you to make sure he or she heard and understood it.* This can be done very simply, and often fairly casually: "I want you to tell me what you're going to do tonight."

Other ways of making this request are:

"Okay, repeat back to me what Daddy wants from you when he's on the telephone talking to his friends."
"What's the rule we talked about when you go out?"

Younger children will usually reply readily, but the middle-to-late adolescent is frequently more defensive and may see you as treating her "like a baby." "I know" or "Do you think I'm retarded?" is a more likely response than a direct reiteration of the expectation. With some teens you can kid or cajole them into repeating it ("Humor me, John. Tell me again what I want you to do" or "Do you remember what I asked of you?"), although more resistant or difficult teens may not be easily kidded or cajoled into repeating the expectation.

4. *Tell the child what the consequences will be for both compliance and noncompliance.* Not only can you use praise for repeating back the expectation ("That's right, Liz, that's exactly what I expect. You've got a good memory."), but you can then let her know what the consequences will be for meeting your expectations.

"If you sleep the whole night in your own bed, tomorrow we'll play together at the park."
"If you play while Daddy's on the phone, there will be a special treat for you after I hang up. But if you interrupt me, you will have to go to time-out after I'm finished."
"If you tell me the truth about where you're going, you'll be able to continue to go out with your friends. If you don't tell the truth, you won't be able to go anywhere."

Everything is very clear and aboveboard. The child knows what you expect, understands it, and is now well aware of what the consequences are for compliance and noncompliance. There is only one thing left for you to. And for many parents, this could be the hardest part.

5. *Follow through.* In order to be effective, you must follow through. There are several aspects to being a parent who is both consistent and firm while following through. You have to remember what your expectation is and monitor whether your child complied with it. You also have to recall what the stated consequences were and make sure that you administer both positive and negative consequences.

Some parents think that just telling their child what the rule or expectation is should elicit compliance because she "should" go along with it without any further problem. However, it's not likely that a problem, whether minor or more serious, will be handled that easily. Children must be taught and trained to comply and to change their behavior.

This 5-Step Method of Increasing Compliance is one way of doing such training. The beauty of this procedure is that it allows you to put the three discipline techniques for encouraging desired and expected behavior into the proper perspective so they can be used effectively and with a purpose in mind.

Summary

Reminder Praise is a way of praising children and teenagers while also reminding them of what they are not (and should not be) doing.

1. **Reminder Praise, like other forms of reinforcement, should be used during or immediately after a desired behavior. It requires that you use such phrases as "and not," "instead of," "rather than," or "without."**
2. **Reminder Praise must be used only when children are not misbehaving. They must be doing something positive while avoiding a previous problem behavior.**

3. **The connector words in Reminder Praise are essential to its success so the child knows you are noticing his or her improvement.**

Three examples of Reminder Praise are:

"You asked me for help without whining or demanding."

"Thanks for being so quiet when you came in the house and not stomping up the steps."

"Great! You saved some of your allowance instead of spending it all. I'm proud of you."

Reminder Praise can be combined with Rewards and Privileges.

The 5-Step Method of Increasing Compliance is a way of letting kids know your expectations, communicating the consequences for compliance and noncompliance, and checking your own ability to follow through with stated consequences.

The 5 steps are:

1. **Identify the problem.**
2. **State your expectations.**
3. **Ask the child to repeat your expectations.**
4. **Tell the child the consequences of compliance and noncompliance with the expectation.**
5. **Follow through.**

Homework Assignment for Week 4

I. Use the 5-Step Method of Increasing Compliance at least five times during the week. To help you to do this, fill in the blanks in the outline that follows:

1. Identify the problem.
   The problem that concerns me is this: ——————————

Stating this problem in a positive way, the expectation I have is this: I expect that my child will: ———————

2. Tell your child your expectation.
   When I stated my expectation to my child, this is what I said: ————————————————————————

3. Ask the child to repeat the expectation back to you.
   When I asked my child to repeat the expectation back to me, my child said: ——————————————————

4. Tell your child the consequences of compliance and non-compliance.
   I selected the following positive consequence if she met my expectation: ———————————————————

   I decided the following negative consequence would take place if my child didn't meet my expectation: ————————

   I told my child about the positive and negative consequences in the following way: ———————————————

5. Follow through.
   Follow through with this procedure is extremely important. Describe how you followed through with your child: ———

II. While using the 5-Step Method of Increasing Compliance, you probably had many opportunities to use Reminder Praise and other discipline techniques for bringing about desired and expected behaviors. Describe the ways you have used:

1. Reminder Praise: ————————————————

2. Rewards and Privileges: ————————————————

   ——————————————————————————

3. Praise and Attention: ————————————————

   ——————————————————————————

8.

Week 5: Discouraging Misbehaviors by Withdrawing Attention

By Week 5—the beginning of the second half of the 8-week program—many parents are feeling fairly comfortable using the discipline techniques that reinforce desired and appropriate behaviors.

Mary Cole said she used the 5-Step Method of Increasing Compliance with her younger son, Randy, to encourage him to bring schoolbooks home. "I don't know that it changed Randy's behavior," Mary said to the class, "but I felt I knew how to handle it when he failed to bring his books home from school. Before I was too angry."

Gail Hackett added that she used both Reminder Praise and the 5-Step Method with her children. "Letting them know what I wanted from them in a calm and direct way helped. Then, when they complied, I used Praise and Reminder Praise. For the first time, I felt as if I had a plan for how to respond to the good and not so good things my kids are doing."

"I've used everything we've studied so far," said Rita Carmichael, "but I have a question. What do you do if your daughter did something you didn't like? Shouldn't you say something?"

She had us set up. We couldn't resist hearing the rest of the story, and Pete Hernandez directed her to "explain yourself."

"Well, it's like this," Rita continued. "Amber was talking on the phone yesterday after a girlfriend called her. Only she didn't remember that the answering machine records conversations if you don't answer before the third ring. I wasn't there at the time, but when I came home and replayed messages I heard my daughter— the same one who came home from school last year telling me she wanted to live in a profanity-free household—using a filthy word. She certainly didn't hear that word at home.

"My question is this: Should I scold her for using this kind of profanity?"

Rita had unintentionally provided the perfect lead-in to a discussion of the main topic of Week 5: how to determine when to deal with a child's behavior and when to ignore it. This is the point at which the introduction of an important new discipline technique—Ignoring Behavior—is especially useful to parents.

A Discipline Technique to Reduce Unwanted Behavior

It would be wonderful if I could tell you that just by continuing to use the discipline techniques presented so far, you'll find your kids gradually getting better and better while the behavior you dislike fades away.

I can't say that, though. There are still more discipline skills to be learned and added to your total approach to raising children: the techniques that assist you to eliminate or to diminish unwanted behaviors. Weeks 5 through 7 focus on learning and practicing these methods.

I suppose there are some lucky parents who have such an easy time raising their children with Praise and Attention, Rewards and Privileges, and Reminder Praise that they never have to resort to other techniques. Most of us, however, are not that fortunate. We have to ignore many irritating behaviors and use punishment to deal with seriously undesirable behaviors. These are the techniques to be discussed in the next few chapters.

In the groups I conduct, parents are very eager to get to the second half of the 8-week program because they feel the more "punitive" techniques will give them a better handle on how to stop troublesome behavior.

In most classes, it's usually during the first or second session that one or more parents say something like this: "Yeah, praise and all that is okay, but my kid is swearing at me. Do you expect me to ignore that?"

Another typical comment in an early session is: "What am I supposed to do if you say we can't use punishment yet? Isn't this just saying that they can do whatever they want?"

I have found that it's a mistake to allow parents to use the techniques introduced in the latter half of the course too quickly. It becomes, I fear, too easy for parents to rely on the discipline skills that discourage inappropriate behavior while assuming that skills like Praise and Attention, Rewards and Privileges, and Reminder Praise just won't work well with their child. In fact they won't, if you're not fully committed to using and practicing them regularly.

Granted, heaping praise on our kids and giving rewards won't solve all problems, but neither will more punitive techniques. It is, I believe, the use of a combination of techniques—without relying on any one way of approaching the problems and challenges that face you—that makes all the difference.

So it's important to continue the positive skills you've practiced in the first few weeks of trying to bring about change in your child or adolescent's behavior. Go on using methods that enhance self-esteem and strengthen behavior you want. Now, though, you will begin to add other skills to your parenting kit of useful discipline methods. Always keep in mind, however, that the techniques that have been introduced so far are the only ones that will bring about new behavior or reinforce existing but weak behavior.

The group of discipline skills that come next cannot do that. They can help to weaken or eliminate undesired behavior, but they never teach or reinforce the kinds of behavior you would rather see instead. So don't get too comfortable with these techniques. Do not come to rely heavily on them in dealing with your kids.

They are available to use as needed and to employ when Praise and Attention, Rewards and Privileges, and Reminder Praise aren't bringing about the results you would like.

Active Intervener Parents

It is my observation that many parents who have child behavior difficulties are what might be called "Active Interveners." That is, they believe that unwanted behavior and troublesome actions of their children just cannot be ignored. Something always has to be done. If not, they fear, they are reinforcing an undesired behavior.

"If I let him get away with it this time, he'll think he can get away with it every time" is one of the arguments of Active Interveners.

"You're not asking us to just ignore bad behavior, are you?" Active Interveners always ask during early weeks of the program. Although I prefer to save a full discussion of the technique of Ignoring Misbehavior for Week 5, in fact parents do have to ignore some of the bad behavior in the first four weeks of this program while they are practicing the techniques introduced so far.

If you are using Praise, for example, you have to wait until the appropriate and desired behavior occurs. For example, if you have a disrespectful, demanding child who says demeaning things to you when she doesn't get her way quickly enough, the only time you can use praise is after she has approached you in a more courteous way. When she has said, "Mom, could I please play with Patricia?" you can praise her for asking in the right way. And if she accepts a "No, dinner's almost ready" with an "Okay," you can further comment about her calm behavior. However, you cannot use praise if she approaches you with the behavior you don't like. You have to wait for the praiseworthy behavior to happen.

For many parents, especially Active Interveners, waiting is difficult. They are impatient. They want results now, not five years from now. But, as I emphasized in the first three chapters, it is my strong belief, based on sound research, that children develop behavior problems when parents inadvertently reinforce misbehavior by actively responding to it. Most parents experiencing difficulties with their children need to learn a little more patience.

Let me give a couple of examples of Active Intervener parents. One is a mother who stated in no uncertain terms that she couldn't ignore her child's behavior. "He gets in my face," she said, "and makes me pay attention to him."

This mother cites being on the phone as a time when her son bothers her until she's angry. "It's not fair," she said. "I can't even talk on the telephone without him bothering me, but I don't know what to do about it. I can't stand it when he's constantly interrupting me when I'm talking." She said she tried to handle this by getting angry, covering the mouthpiece of the phone, and shouting at her son to "leave me alone until I'm finished."

Pete Hernandez was another Active Intervener. He was also adamant: "I just won't have Valerie swearing in my house!"

Valerie had a knack, Pete admitted to the other parents, for pushing all of his wrong buttons. If Valerie didn't get her way, she would verbally harass him until Pete was fuming. The latest incident occurred when Valerie asked to have a girlfriend spend the night.

Pete said that would be okay as long as Valerie's friend came over after Pete had returned home from grocery shopping, around eight o'clock that evening. Valerie found that unacceptable and told him so. Pete calmly explained his reasons, but this didn't satisfy the persistent Valerie.

"I don't see why she can't come over now," wailed Valerie in a tone of voice that never failed to irritate her father.

"I gave you the reasons and that's that," replied Pete.

"But why can't I have Janet over now? Why don't you ever like my friends? Don't you trust us?"

The harangue went on, and Pete, who tried to stay calm and in control, felt himself getting more angry and frustrated. Valerie started sulking and went to her room only to return within seconds. She intensified the verbal assault and finally used her trump card: "You're nothing but a stupid fascist who won't let me do anything," she screamed.

The wrong button had finally been pushed, and Pete grabbed Valerie by the collar, pushing her toward her room. Valerie fell and began crying and calling her father more unpleasant names.

In discussing this incident later, Pete again stated that nothing bothered him as much as being screamed at and called names by his daughter. "I'll always react that way," he insisted. "If I don't, she'll think she got away with something and do it all the more."

If this sounds familiar, if you see yourself as an Active Intervener, if you have a low tolerance for frustration or a high level of stress, you may be wondering whether you shouldn't just skip this chapter. Don't yield to this impulse. Instead, stick it out and then decide. As many others in parent-training classes discover, this could well be the most important—albeit the most difficult—segment in the 8-week series. It is certainly a vital link in the whole sequence of learning and applying effective discipline skills.

How Not to Pay Attention to Misbehavior

Ignoring Behavior means that you systematically do not respond to the behavior you wish to eliminate. You do not flinch, grimace, smile, tense your facial muscles, mumble under your breath, slam cupboard doors, or walk out of a room quickly. As soon as the misbehavior begins, you switch off any overt response to it. When it ends, you respond to appropriate behavior or continue normal interaction and conversation.

To ignore behavior is hardly a passive exercise, as some parents (especially Active Interveners) may think at first. On the contrary, to do it correctly requires not only remarkable self-restraint, but also the consistent withholding of responses to the unwanted behavior.

Two sets of parents in one of my parent-training classes demonstrated the challenge of holding back responses from children's behavior.

Ben and Glynis Goldman told one class that their fourteen-year-old daughter, Sandra, was "obnoxious and disagreeable." She was flippant, sarcastic, and often mean-spirited with her parents. It was not uncommon for Sandra to say "I hate you" or "You make me sick" to them if they invoked a rule or told her no when she wanted to use the phone or go to a friend's house.

Both of Sandra's parents are Active Interveners. They said they couldn't help responding to her nasty words. "See? See the way she talks to me?" Ben would say to his wife. Glynis usually reminded Sandra how disrespectful she was being and how that hurt both her mother and her father. When she became angry about it, Glynis would say, "Don't you dare talk to me like that. Who do you think I am? A piece of dirt that you can wipe your feet on?"

None of these comments changed Sandra's behavior. She remained disrespectful and sarcastic to her parents, and there were frequent arguments in the household about what she had said to them, often escalating to name-calling and slammed doors.

In another family, eight-year-old Kevin was called in from play in the backyard when his lunch was ready. "I fixed chicken noodle soup and ham sandwiches," his mother said. "Wash your hands and come eat."

"I hate chicken noodle soup," Kevin said, making a face as he walked toward the bathroom. "Why do you always fix things I don't like?"

In a few seconds, far too short a time for his hands to be really scrubbed, Kevin returned to the kitchen and sat at the counter to eat lunch.

"Can I have potato chips?" asked Kevin.

"No," said his mother. "If you have some now, there won't be enough for anyone else and I planned to have them for dinner tonight with the hot dogs."

"You're so mean," grumbled Kevin as he ate his chicken noodle soup.

"You really have a good appetite today," his mother noted cheerfully.

In these two vignettes, the parents handled their children's behavior in different ways. The Goldmans were Active Interveners who couldn't avoid making comments about their daughter's behavior because it was so distressing to them. In contrast to this way of handling a child's verbal behaviors was Kevin's mother's method. Kevin obviously displayed behavior that his mother found unappealing. Yet she knew Kevin well enough to understand that his frequent complaints, objections, and even refusals didn't amount to much more than verbalizations. While she wished he would be more pleasant, agreeable, and cooperative in his comments, she did not pay his grumpiness attention. To do so, she figured, would make it worse.

Kevin's mother is probably right. When undesired behaviors—verbal or otherwise—receive attention, they usually occur more often. This is what has happened between Pete and Valerie, as well as with Sandra and her parents, the Goldmans. Both Ben and Glynis Goldman and Pete always criticized, scolded, or punished their child's behavior. Yet the behavior did not improve or stop. At the same time, these parents believed that "doing nothing" would reinforce the things they couldn't accept.

The Appropriate Ways to Ignore Behavior

Any response to whining, crying, demanding, hyperactive, impulsive, or uncooperative behavior (to name a few of the behaviors parents usually want to eliminate) with scolding, nagging, complaints, or punishment may make those behaviors stronger, not weaker. The premise of Ignoring Behavior is to withhold *all* attention from the behaviors to be stopped.

The key to the effective use of the technique is to do it *systematically.* You cannot eliminate a behavior by haphazardly or occasionally ignoring it. Only through systematic, consistent, and ongoing ignoring will you succeed. In fact, if you pay attention to a behavior on some occasions and not on others, you could be reinforcing the behavior.

Six-year-old Ryan Franklin bit other children at school, refused to stay in his seat in the classroom, swore at his mother when he was angry, and often failed to do what he was told at home or elsewhere. When his mother began to apply Ignoring Behavior, she was concerned that it wouldn't be effective.

"I've tried ignoring him," Nancy Franklin said, "but it doesn't work. He keeps up the same behavior or follows me around the house until I can't take it any more."

Parents who are beginning to learn about how to apply Ignoring Behavior almost always say they have tried it and "it doesn't work with my kid." What this often means is that they've tried it briefly without knowing the guidelines for its use and without supervision. When it didn't produce fairly quick results, they gave it up to try something else.

What parents don't always recognize is that Ignoring Behavior can be a very taxing discipline technique to employ. In the case of Ryan Franklin, he was undeniably a difficult child who demanded attention from his mother as well as from teachers. To ignore him was like sentencing him to solitary confinement, something he could not tolerate well at all. He liked having the attention and the responses of adults. When a teacher or his mother attempted to ignore him, he would become a compulsive talker or question-asker. "Why are you ignoring me, Mom? How come you're not talking to me? Don't walk away from me! If you don't answer me, I'll hold my breath!" Nancy Franklin found that even locking herself in the bathroom wasn't an easy way to ignore Ryan; he would stand outside the door and cry, scream, shout, or kick the door.

It would have helped Nancy to realize that for most children or teens, when certain behaviors are ignored, they get worse at first. Knowing this ahead of time makes a world of difference. When you can predict that the behaviors you are trying to eliminate will get worse before they get better, you will be more inclined to hang in there with the difficult behaviors.

Why Is Ignoring Behavior Important?

Why is it so vital to learn how to Ignore? It's not only because we have to stop reacting to unwanted behavior. There's another important reason, which has to do with combining discipline techniques. Using the technique of Ignoring in combination with the techniques that serve to reinforce behavior and with some methods of punishment makes each discipline technique you employ that much more effective.

In Weeks 3 and 4 of this program, when I introduced Rewards and Privileges and Reminder Praise, I mentioned the value of combining praise with a reward or adding a reward or privilege to Reminder Praise. When you do this, you are stringing together, or combining, discipline techniques. It is essential if you are to deal with children and teens successfully that you not only string techniques together but learn to separate behavioral events in your thinking.

Many, if not most, mothers and fathers tend to think in general ways about their kids' behavior. When reviewing a youngster's day or week, they may think of him or her as either "good" or "bad." This more global way of remembering a child's behavior can be advantageous for the youngster if Mom forgets the sarcasm and recalls only the several helpful things he or she did. On the other hand, it can be a serious problem if Dad, looking back on the week, completely forgets the times when his child was cooperative and pleasant, remembering only that he or she forgot to cut the lawn, complained about not getting enough privileges, and had a tantrum when told he had to go to a family reunion. To use discipline effectively, however, it is essential to discard generalizations and respond to specific behaviors.

Each behavior, no matter how minor or major, can be looked at as a specific event for which there may be a specific discipline. In truth, most behavior doesn't have too much to do with what came before or will come after. Children quickly forget what they did a few minutes or an hour ago, and they definitely want to be judged only by their most recent actions.

Take a situation contributed by Judi Perna during a class. Four-year-old Jerry is playing in the same room with his two-year-old sister. He snatches a toy away from her and she cries. A few minutes later, tired of the toy, he returns it to her. She smiles. Jerry then asks his mother for permission to go outside. Outside, he taunts another child, but later he is riding down the sidewalk on his bike next to this same boy.

Watching all of this, Judi cannot say that her son is a "good," "bad," angry, maladjusted, or optimistic child. All she can say about the sequence is that Jerry is a boy who did some things that she approved and some things she would like to discourage. If she were to respond to Jerry's behaviors, she would handle each of them in a different way.

That is the way it should be; there should be no carry-over from one behavior to another. Each behavior should have its own response. It would be very confusing to Jerry if his mother waited until the several behaviors mentioned were over before she decided to punish him for being so selfish and uncooperative with his young sister. Jerry probably wouldn't know what she was talking about. Similarly, if she told him he was "always so good and kind to others," he might be equally mixed up.

I've emphasized so far that the positive techniques covered in Weeks 1 through 4 should be used during or immediately following a behavior you wish to strengthen. You may now see an excellent reason for this: Children's behavior changes like the weather in the Midwest. It is unpredictable and whimsical. Deal with it before it changes, because if nothing else is certain, you can be sure it will change.

If you can separate each behavior from the one before or after and deal with each as it comes along, you will be in a better position to string various discipline techniques together.

That's where Ignoring Behavior comes in. Because you can't respond with more active discipline techniques to every action of your child, knowing how and when to Ignore Behavior is extremely useful. Applying the technique properly enables you to "do something."

You Can't Ignore Everything

It is also important for parents to have an idea about which behaviors to respond to with other disciplinary actions and which ones to ignore. "You can't ignore everything," parents in groups protest. I agree. So how do you decide which ones to ignore?

One rule of thumb is to look at which misbehaviors seem to be intended to gain your attention. Any attention-getting behavior ought to be ignored. This might include tattling, sibling fighting, whining, demanding, crying, swearing, throwing tantrums, and hitting. Even with teenagers, as most experienced parents realize, sarcasm, back talk, and complaining are often meant to goad us or provoke us, or are a way of trying out a new role for the teen.

Additional serious candidates for Ignoring include minor irritating, obnoxious, and annoying behaviors. Even if you have a child or adolescent with severe behavior problems, chances are that a lot of his or her behavior is simply irritating, and annoying. You must make a decision about which behavior to respond to and which to ignore.

What are the behaviors you should pay attention to? Just the desirable, appropriate, and positive behaviors, along with the serious or dangerous misbehaviors. We can't ignore an action that will hurt a child or another person, one that is against the law, or one that will destroy valuable property. For the most part, those behaviors are the exception rather than the rule. Generally, the behaviors that most annoy parents are (or at least start out as) minor and not so serious.

When Rita's thirteen-year-old used the offensive word in the recorded telephone conversation, she was probably not trying to get her mother's attention or annoy her, since she was unaware that the conversation was being taped. More likely, it was a response to her own need to fit in with her peers. Because she wasn't swearing at her mother and had in the past requested a "profanity-free house," her behavior is the kind that can safely be ignored.

Knowing that Ignoring Behavior is a difficult technique to use and that the behavior ignored is likely to get worse before it gets better will be helpful to you. Another thing you should know to use this skill effectively is that you must be consistent. Each time the behavior occurs—say, complaining about what you have prepared for lunch (as Kevin did)—it must be ignored. Don't withhold attention one time and then angrily react to it another time.

Certainly you don't want to teach your child that if he or she is persistent enough, you will cave in and respond. That's what Ryan's mother tends to do when his carrying on becomes too obnoxious to bear. Granted, Ryan is a very persistent and difficult boy. However, if you use this technique to combat an unwanted behavior, then be prepared to stick to your guns.

Finding Ways of Coping with Your Stress

Sticking to your guns may mean that you need to find ways of dealing with that persistent kid who is likely to test your resolve. For many parents this will include learning new coping strategies for keeping your cool in the face of extreme pressure.

If you are an Active Intervener, have low tolerance for frustration, or lose your patience fairly quickly, then you might try one of these suggestions:

- Try a deep breathing exercise or learn another relaxation technique. When you're stressed, breathing usually becomes fast and shallow. You can ease stress by consciously practicing a more relaxed way of breathing.
- Tune out any other people around you if you are not home alone or if you are in a public place. Don't respond with ineffectual or harmful discipline methods just because others are watching you.

Finding Ways of Coping with Your Stress (cont.)

- Turn on some soothing music or sing softly to yourself. Classical music or other tranquil forms of music or sounds (such as a recording of the ocean waves) can be relaxing.
- Call someone on the telephone for support or write about your feelings or problems. Putting thoughts into words helps your mind organize overwhelming situations.
- Adopt a saying that makes sense for you to remember or repeat to yourself. In other words, find a focus word. Think of a word that suggests tranquillity— something like "peace," "calm," or "ocean." Repeat the word to yourself at a relaxed pace; fit it rhythmically with your slowed-down breathing.
- Do some quiet reading of a favorite book or an exciting novel; try a good parenting book; or look at your child's baby album.
- Work out with physical exercise; aerobics or even vigorously cleaning the house can reduce stress. Moving around can break the tension, but sustained aerobic exercise works best.
- Use a Parent Time-Out; tell your kid you need a time-out away from him for fifteen or thirty minutes.

Using one or more of such methods to reduce stress and pressure can help you remain in control and withstand your youngster's attempt to get your attention. Also helpful is to keep track of the length of time the unwanted behavior persists when you ignore it. Keeping a chart of the number of minutes it lasts or the times it occurs can help you detach yourself enough to continue to remain controlled and patient.

When the Misbehavior Ends, Combine Ignoring with Other Techniques

When the misbehavior does end (temporarily or permanently), combine Ignoring Behavior with another technique. Consider using Reminder Praise, for instance, in the following way: "You got control of yourself without my punishing you. I like that."

Or: "You stopped hitting your sister without my speaking to you. Great job!"

Summary

Ignoring Behavior is a very valuable discipline technique to use with misbehavior. It should be considered for use with misbehaviors that are minor, irritating, obnoxious, annoying, or directed at getting your attention.

Remember that it is very difficult at first for many parents to ignore misbehavior, but with practice it becomes easier.

As soon as the unwanted or undesirable behavior begins, start ignoring it. To truly ignore a behavior, do not respond to it in any way. As soon as the unwanted behavior stops, cease ignoring and begin to respond to appropriate behavior with Praise and Attention, Rewards and Privileges, Reminder Praise, or just normal talk and communication.

If a child's behavior is very annoying, irritating, or upsetting, consider using some form of relaxation or other calm-inducing coping strategies to help you remain in control and to avoid giving in and responding to the misbehavior.

Homework Assignment for Week 5

The homework assignment for this week is to use Ignoring Behavior to reduce or eliminate an undesirable behavior. Select a troublesome behavior that meets at least one criterion (atten-

tion-getting, minor, irritating, annoying, or obnoxious), and write this behavior here: —————————————————————

———————————————————————————————————

Understand and remember that the behavior may get worse before it gets better and that it may be very difficult for you to ignore behavior that is obnoxious or causes you stress. Decide what coping strategies you might use if you have trouble ignoring. Write one or more potential coping strategies here:

1. ————————————————————————————

———————————————————————————————————

———————————————————————————————————

2. ————————————————————————————

———————————————————————————————————

———————————————————————————————————

3. ————————————————————————————

———————————————————————————————————

———————————————————————————————————

Ignore the selected behavior each time it occurs. Record the number of times you ignore it by placing check marks in the space for each day below:

MONDAY: —————————————————————————

TUESDAY: ————————————————————————

WEDNESDAY: ———————————————————————

THURSDAY: ———————————————————————

FRIDAY:—————————————————————————

SATURDAY: ———————————————————————

SUNDAY: —————————————————————————

Remember that many behaviors won't diminish in just a week. Plan to continue to use Ignoring Behavior even after this week is up.

9.

Week 6: Effective Punishment to Discourage Problem Behaviors

I t works," said Ron Morgan at the beginning of the sixth class. Ron told the group of parents that during the last week he'd used a new technique with Kurt, his nine-year-old son. "I used Ignoring and it worked right away. I didn't think that would happen."

Ron explained that he had had lots of conflicts and arguments with Kurt. But after last week's class, he decided to use Ignoring Behavior instead. "When I stopped paying attention to some of the little annoying things he does—like making strange noises and talking while I'm watching TV—he stopped doing those things and left the room. And I didn't have to say anything to him."

Ron Morgan also was eager to tell the class how he used one other technique he had learned. Following the last class, Ron and his wife, Jean, decided to use the 5-Step Method of Increasing Compliance to help Kurt finish schoolwork at home.

"It actually kind of fell into place," Jean said as she picked up on the story. "Both my husband and Kurt love basketball, and Ron got some tickets to a Pistons game. I stayed out of it, and Ron really handled it well. He told Kurt that he expected his homework to be done before they went to the game. He said that if his homework wasn't done, then Kurt would have to stay home."

Ron added that he followed all the steps of the procedure as they were outlined in the class. But when it was time to go, Kurt had not finished his homework. "I said to him very calmly," Ron said, "'I'm sorry, Kurt, but I told you what would happen if you didn't finish your work. No game.'"

Jean said that Kurt put up a fuss, but Ron didn't give in or feel guilty. "Why should I?" said Ron in class. "I gave him every chance, didn't I?" So he stood firm, and a disappointed Kurt stayed home.

Ron enjoyed the confidence he felt in doing this, but the biggest payoff came about two days later. "Kurt came up to me about two nights after this happened and told me that he knew why I didn't let him go the game. 'It was for my own good, wasn't it, Dad?' Can you beat that? I thought he was going to be mad at me, but instead he seemed to like it better when I stuck to what I said."

The lesson Ron learned is clear: when we stick to what we say and act in a self-confident way with our children, they are more likely to appreciate what we're doing for them.

This doesn't mean that Ignoring Behavior is the best way to deal with every action we'd like to keep our children from doing. Week 6 gives parents additional tools for discouraging or eliminating misbehavior.

Consider these three situations:

Four-year-old Aaron seemed to beg for punishment, his mother, Tamara Blakely, told a group of parents. One day Aaron was hitting his two-year-old brother as well as the puppy. Tamara thought it was deliberate. She sent him to sit in a chair in the corner for five minutes.

After his few minutes of Time-Out were served, Aaron made a beeline for his brother, who was playing quietly, and slapped him. Tamara, caught short by this behavior, shouted, "Aaron, what are you doing? You're back on the time-out chair, young man."

The same thing happened after the second Time-Out, and the third. Exasperated, his mother finally sent him to his room for the afternoon. In the class she explained, "I had to do something different, because time-out wasn't working. How can it be working if he keeps doing the same thing over and over?"

Nancy Klein attended another parent-training class. She told about an arrangement she had with her fourteen-year-old daughter, Missy. When they were at an amusement park, Nancy told the class, Missy was to check in at a designated spot every hour. All went well until the last check-in time prior to leaving for the night. Missy didn't show up. Nancy and her son waited impatiently and then began to look for Missy.

When they finally found her two hours later, Nancy was both frightened and furious. "Where were you?" she asked Missy. "How come you didn't check in as you were supposed to?"

Missy's weak excuse was that she forgot to look at her watch and she was having too much fun with some kids from school she met.

There was little conversation as they drove home. At home, though, Nancy told Missy that she was grounded for the rest of the weekend even though they all had planned to return to the park the next day.

Missy was upset. "I told the kids that I would see them tomorrow. They'll be looking for me."

"I don't care," replied Nancy. "You agreed to check in every hour and you didn't do that. I'm grounding you to teach you a lesson."

"I don't care what you say," said Missy. "I'm going anyway. You promised we'd spend the weekend there and you can't make me stay home."

Nancy was remarkably calm as she said, "It's up to you. If you leave here tomorrow, there will be further consequences."

The next day there was no further discussion of the subject, and Missy did not appear as upset as Nancy imagined she might be. When Nancy asked her daughter to go grocery shopping with her in the afternoon, Missy agreed. As Nancy recalled this incident in the class, she remarked that they had a good time, and after loading the groceries in the car went to an ice cream shop for a sinful dessert.

"I don't know why Missy let it drop," she said to the other parents.

"Maybe it was because you didn't fight with her and didn't threaten her," one of the other parents suggested. "You sounded really calm and self-confident. As if you knew what you were doing."

"I wish I felt that way more often with Missy," Nancy commented.

In the same class with Nancy Klein was a father who told about his young son Jake. After Tim Johnson had spanked five-year-old Jake for the fifth time in two days, this time for disobeying his father's rule about spitting, a defiant Jake looked at his father and said: "Someday I'm going to be bigger than you. When I am, you're going to be sorry. I'm going to spank you just like you spanked me. See how you like it!"

For several days after that, Jake ate all his vegetables without being told in order to grow up faster and be big and strong like his father. Tim thought it was cute at the time and told several friends about it.

"Do you suppose he'll really remember this when he's older?" Tim's neighbor asked him. "Maybe you should go easy on spanking him."

"My father spanked me, and I turned out all right, didn't I?" queried Tim rhetorically.

In the class that Tim attended, however, he wasn't so sure anymore. "Do you suppose Jake really will try to get even with me?" he asked the other parents.

It is safe to say that children don't just need more punishment. What they do require, though, is more effective punishment. There's a difference between more or harsher punishment and effective punishment.

Effective Punishment

What is punishment? For our purposes, we can say that punishment is a penalty administered by a parent to discourage present or future misbehavior. There is considerable research that suggests that punishments can be highly effective when given correctly, and that sometimes punishment works better than discipline that relies on positive reinforcement.

Two of the characteristics of successful and effective parents, as mentioned in Chapter 4 ("Week 1: The 12 Keys to Effective Parenting"), are consistency and firmness. Consistency is critical to every discipline technique mentioned so far, and it is just as important to the effective use of punishment. Firmness, however, almost always relates more to punishment than to some other discipline techniques.

When I introduce the topic of punishment in Week 6 of my parent-training courses, I ask for parents to share their thoughts about what makes for good punishment. Someone always suggests "sticking to your punishment." That is firmness. And there is no question that to make punishment work, parents must "stick to it." That is perhaps why Nancy Klein's punishment seemed to work well with Missy. And it may be a reason why four-year-old Aaron's punishment was not so effective.

There are, however, several other factors that make for successful punishment. Those factors are:

- Timing
- Severity
- Fairness
- Frequency
- Follow-through
- Reasoning
- Context

If you take these factors into consideration when you punish a child or adolescent, your use of punishment should be more successful. But you need to know more about each of these critical factors.

Timing

Timing may not be everything in punishment, but it can be very important in several ways. Generally speaking, the more immediate the punishment, the more effective it will be.

There are some good reasons for this. One is that when you're dealing with small children, especially, the sooner the punishment takes place the easier it is for the youngster to make a connection between the punishment and the misbehavior.

Another reason relates to something brought up in the last chapter: kids' behavior changes—sometimes fairly rapidly. No child is bad all the time. In quick succession a child will do something mean, then angelic, then infuriating. So if you want to avoid confusing your child about the connection between the punishment and the unwanted behavior, punish before the next desirable behavior occurs.

This is especially useful to keep in mind if you're inclined to delay your punishment only to find your kid doing something so irresistibly appealing that you feel guilty about following through with a negative consequence.

Severity

While the shortest good-byes might be the best (at least in the movies), neither the shortest nor the longest punishments are necessarily the best in healthy families.

A punishment that is too short is lax. Lax punishments have no impact and can be virtually the same as no punishment at all.

Harsh, overly long, or severe infliction of pain or suffering is also ineffective. While strong punishments may temporarily stop the misbehavior in question, they can produce unwanted side effects. Most common among the side effects of overly harsh punishment are hostility and resentment.

Parents find that the results of extreme punishment are not at all what they desire. For one thing, what we want children to do when we punish them is to reflect on what they have done wrong, feel guilt, and make a decision to improve their behavior. The goal for parents is not to vent their own anger, bring about compliance because of fear of the parents' power, or create a submissive or anxious child. The main idea is to help the child understand that there are unpleasant consequences for misbehavior.

When punishment is too harsh, an opposite reaction takes place. The child's focus is removed from the misdeed and centered on the punisher. This happened with five-year-old Jake Johnson. Jake's father was pleased that his son became obedient for a few days after their encounter. But Jake was hardly looking inward and reflecting on what he did wrong. Rather, he was concentrating on growing up to be big and strong so he could get even with his father.

In other words, when children experience harsh punishment, they look outward to the person who inflicted the punishment and blame that person—often, like Jake, vowing to get revenge.

Fairness

The punishment should fit the crime. When little misbehaviors that deserve punishment take place, they should be given little punishments. When the punishment is an overreaction to the offense, it leaves the child considering the unfairness—again taking the emphasis away from the misbehavior—and it puts the parent in a difficult position for the future. What are they going to use for punishment when a major offense occurs if they've already used their ultimate weapons?

Kids are especially keen to note unfairness. If a sibling gets more or less of a punishment for the same offense, or if a punishment is not suited to the problem, kids will be quick to let you know. It's the parent's responsibility to make sure that the punishment is as fair as possible.

But this isn't always easy, and you can't please your kids all the time—particularly when punishment is the issue. Some parents have tried to resolve this by asking the child what he or she thinks is an appropriate punishment. Others are willing to negotiate. In the end, the parent has to settle on something. Here are some examples of unfair punishments contributed by people in some of my parent-training classes, along with more equitable punishments:

Misbehavior	Unfair Punishment	Fair Punishment
Swearing	Washing out mouth with strong soap	Verbal reprimand
Stealing	Restricting child to room for three weeks	Working off amount stolen
Playing music too loud	Taking away CD player for two weeks	Restricting use of CD player for one night
Fighting	Spanking and grounding	Reprimand and warning
Low grades	Restricting child to house for six weeks	Restricting telephone calls during study time

It is important that you make every possible effort to be fair. Sometimes it's useful to discuss this with other parents so that you have more objective opinions about the fairness of your punishments.

Frequency

Punishment works best when it is infrequent. Otherwise, children become immune to its effects. This is true of most things in life: the more often we are exposed to favorite foods, loud noises, scary movies, or punishments, the more used to them we become and the less power or meaning they have. Children learn to deal with punishment—even if it is painful or severe. If punishment is inflicted only on rare occasions, it will have a bigger impact on children.

If punishments should be infrequent, they should nonetheless be consistent. That means that if you have decided to punish a specific behavior, then every time that behavior occurs it ought to be followed by punishment. But if a behavior is happening often (say that Aaron, mentioned above, is hitting, slapping, or pinching his younger brother several times a day), the punishment might well have to be frequent.

There is a way around this apparent dilemma. I said earlier that only serious or dangerous misbehavior should be on your list of things that deserve punishment. Sticking to that guideline is one way to limit the frequency of punishment. The other is to restrict punishment to one type of misbehavior at a time. For instance, if you are punishing a child's aggressiveness against her baby brother, then at the same time, and until the problem is cleared up, you should make that the only behavior to receive punishment.

Follow-Through

Follow-through is important in punishment in several ways. First, if you use a warning or threat (often a part of punishment), then you must always carry it out if the misbehavior occurs. Never give a warning or threat you're not fully prepared to carry out. If a child chooses to call your bluff or to test the limits, then follow through with the punishment. This was a factor in Missy Klein's situation, described at the beginning of this chapter. By her calm and deliberate statement, Karen Klein showed that she was prepared to give Missy further consequences should she choose to return to the amusement park the next day. Missy decided not to put her mother's resolve to the test.

Second, once a punishment has been given, you must follow through. That means making sure that the child serves the sentence. You must not commute it or let your child talk you out of it. Either will lessen the impact of your future punishments. Earlier, when discussing the severity of punishment, I indicated that a lax one is a weak and ineffective one. When children are able to get out of serving a punishment, that punishment also becomes weak and useless. When you impose punishment, unless you realize it is much too harsh, than the child must serve it. We want children to think about changing their misbehavior, not about how they can escape the consequences of it.

Reasoning

When punishment is accompanied by reasoning, children are helped to understand why their misbehavior is wrong and why it is being punished.

Reasoning—the explanations we give about rules, standards, values, and actions—helps children to understand why misbehavior is being punished. It serves to tell children why we are upset and why we consider a misbehavior serious or dangerous.

One of the most important benefits of reasoning is that it gives children explanations of our punishment (for instance, "When you lie I cannot trust you, and it's very important that we trust each other in this family"). But even more important, reasoning teaches children how to think and gives them a foundation for making decisions on their own. When they know why you believe an action is right or wrong, they will then be able to recall this as they grow older and a parent is not available to guide their behavior.

Context

The context in which punishment takes place is very important. The atmosphere in the family and the relationship between you and your child play a critical role in the effectiveness of punishment.

If the atmosphere is cool or even hostile, the punishment is likely to be taken differently from the way it would be interpreted if there is a generally warm and loving relationship between parent and child. In a less friendly or in a hostile relationship, kids are likely to perceive punishment as meanness, rejection, and hostility on the part of the parent. (Tim Johnson with his frequent spanking of Jake illustrates such a situation.) If this happens, as mentioned above, the youngster will react to the punishment in the wrong way.

We want children not only to accept their punishment but to look inward and decide something like this: "Dad punished me because he loves me and I did something wrong. I have to change my behavior in the future." When punishment takes place in the more critical, negative, and hostile atmosphere, the youngster will react more like this: "Mom is so mean, I hate her. I don't know why she hates me so much. I don't care what she does to me, she's just being mean." So instead of feeling guilty and accepting some blame, the child in a hostile atmosphere will reject the punishment, feel anger rather than guilt, and focus on the punisher instead of on his or her own behavior.

As I wrote in earlier chapters, we always want the focus to be appropriate. For parents the focus should be on the positive and desired behaviors rather than on all the behaviors you dislike. When you focus on the more desired behaviors, you are punishing less often and giving positive reinforcement more often. This leads children to feel you love them, which in turn makes your punishment work well when you sometimes—infrequently, it's hoped—have to punish undesired behavior.

Children and teenagers must have opportunities to earn your approval and to get positive responses from you in a number of ways. If kids can get positive payoffs for alternative, approved behavior, then punishment—even of the mild variety—becomes all the more effective.

You should therefore endeavor to keep all of these factors in mind whenever you believe punishment is called for. If you do, whatever punishment you use will be more likely to have a positive impact.

Reprimands

It is now time to discuss specific types of punishment. The first is a mild punishment called a Reprimand. Most parents have used a scolding (another word for a reprimand), but often it is used in an inexact and sometimes harmful manner.

If you remember the children and the situations introduced at the beginning of this chapter, you can, I'm sure, imagine how a Reprimand or scolding could be used in each situation.

With Aaron, the four-year-old who hit his younger brother, his mother might have been tempted to say such things as the following to him after he was punished but hit his brother again: "Didn't I tell you to stop hitting your brother? That's enough of that! I don't want you to ever hit him again. Do you hear me, young man? That's bad to hit your little brother, and I won't have it! Do you understand?"

Or how about Missy Klein, who didn't show up at the appointed time at the amusement park? Her mother could have launched into this scolding: "How could you do this to us? Do you realize we've been running around this park for two hours looking for you? But do you care? No. Your friends and your own pleasure are more important than your family. You have no consideration for anyone but yourself. Well, I'm sick of it!"

And young Jake Johnson, who vowed revenge toward his father after being spanked for spitting? His father could have said: "That's nasty to spit. I don't want you to ever do that again! Do you hear me? Listen to me when I'm talking to you. That's bad, and anyone who spits is bad."

If any of the three parents had responded in this way, their remarks might qualify as scolding. But they fall short of being considered Reprimands, and they are also not effective punishments.

A Reprimand is a way of letting a child know that you disapprove of a behavior. It is an effective punishment when used infrequently and in a proper way. To give a Reprimand in the right way, it must tell exactly what behavior is undesired and let the child know that you are not pleased with his or her actions.

To return to the three children mentioned above, here are better Reprimands than the ones given before:

To Aaron: "I don't like it when you hit your brother. That hurts him and he feels bad. I don't want you hitting him anymore. I want you to find other ways of solving problems with him."

How to Use Reprimands

Following are two examples of the use of reprimands.

Twelve-year-old David was caught stealing a magazine from the local drugstore, a store where the family frequently shopped. When his mother, Carol Cooper, found out about the theft, she was embarrassed and angry. Soon after David arrived home, she began to talk with him: "I'm very disappointed in you, David. I don't like stealing and it goes against everything we believe in and the principles I've tried to teach you. Furthermore, Mr. Hill, the man who owns the drugstore, has been very kind to us. But he earns his living from the profit he makes on everything he sells, including magazines. When you steal from him, you are stealing his livelihood. That just isn't right. I hope this will never happen again."

Fifteen-year-old Gary had stolen before. His mother, Val Freeman, was a soft-spoken woman who often felt helpless in dealing with Gary's troublesome behavior. After he stole a pair of earring from the next-door neighbor's house, Val was given a quick lesson in using an effective reprimand. She was then ready to confront Gary.

"Gary," she said in a voice that was stronger and more authoritative than her usual quiet, soft voice, "we need to talk." She moved close to him and looked him straight in the eyes and

To Missy: "You agreed to meet us at two o'clock, and you didn't show up. That bothers me when you make an agreement and then fail to live up to it. In the future I expect you to keep agreements we make. To help you remember this, you will not be able to come back to this park tomorrow."

To Jake: "I don't like it when you spit. Please don't do it again. Okay?"

How to Use Reprimands (cont.)

said, "I am very unhappy that you stole a set of earrings from our neighbors. Those are valuable and mean a lot to Mrs. Smith because they were an anniversary gift. I want those earrings returned to me immediately. I'll give you thirty minutes to hand them to me. Do I make myself clear?"

Val was pleasantly surprised that Gary gave her the earrings in less than fifteen minutes. With a newfound sense of confidence about the power she was suddenly feeling, she went with Gary and made him return them personally to Mrs. Smith while offering an apology.

A Reprimand can be delivered in a short, direct statement, as in these examples. I believe that a succinct, right-to-the-point statement is heard and remembered by a child. But there are some other elements of a Reprimand that will make sure it is effective. One is to move closer to the child and to make eye contact. Eye contact must be maintained throughout the Reprimand and held for a few seconds after the verbal part of the Reprimand has ended.

Also, a somewhat louder and more authoritative voice should be used. It is essential that the child know that you mean business. A quiet or weak voice will lessen the effectiveness of this technique.

You can also add reasoning and encouragement to the Reprimand. As mentioned above, reasoning helps to let kids know what behaviors we dislike and why. They can, therefore, be added to a Reprimand. In Aaron's case, reasoning is added when the parent says: "Hitting hurts your brother." In general, as children grow older and are better able to think in more complex ways, reasoning should become more sophisticated. A toddler may not be able to fully empathize with a younger brother's pain yet, but that is a goal and should therefore be used in reasoning.

However, at this age reasoning that includes a reference to avoiding punishment ("If you hit your brother, you will have to go to the Time-Out chair") can be used (the concept of Time-Out is discussed in the next section). As children develop, we also want their thinking and moral reasoning skills to develop as well. Reasoning, then, should be aimed at increasing their ability to empathize and feel for others ("When you didn't show up on time, we were concerned about your safety, and it caused all of us needless worry").

Likewise, encouragement can be added to a Reprimand. Since a Reprimand is a mild punishment, you are inflicting a small amount of pain through your disapproval. You may also wish to impart a positive message. Adding some encouragement is a way to do this. For instance, with five-year-old Jake a parent could Reprimand in this way: "I don't like it when you spit at people. It is not polite to spit at someone else. You are usually very kind to other people, and that's one of the things I like about you. I don't think you want to be mean to others, so I'm very sure that I won't have to remind you about this again."

Reprimands can be used with children of any age and can be highly effective even with a teenager. It is best to avoid using any personal criticism. If the misbehavior is serious, a punishment might be added to it. This is what Nancy Klein did with Missy when she restricted her from returning to the amusement park the next day.

The value of a Reprimand is that it is a verbal punishment that lets kids know exactly what behavior you dislike in a very few short statements. It can be administered and be over with very quickly. As with all punishments, once it is over you do not have to return to the misbehavior or harp on it. You can wrap up a reprimand by saying, "Since we have talked about this, I feel confident that I won't have to speak to you again about hitting your brother." It's useful to do something with the child that shows that the punishment is over by giving your attention for positive behaviors ("So let's play checkers" or "Why don't you help me wash the car?").

Imposing Time-Out

The second type of punishment is Imposing Time-Out. The parents with whom I work find that when they use Time-Out in a consistent manner, it works very well.

Five-year-old Cindy was given Time-Out by her grandmother, Josephine Jennings, after she refused to get out of the pool when her grandmother took her swimming one sweltering summer day.

The next day, Josephine got angry with Cindy because the girl talked back when Josephine told her that they couldn't go swimming again that day. Before Josephine could come up with a punishment, Cindy said, "I'm going to Time-Out now, Grandma."

The stunned grandmother could only say, "That's right, child." But that was the end of talking back for that day.

Cindy clearly accepted Time-Out as an appropriate punishment. So, too, has it become the most acceptable and accepted punishment in homes, schools, foster care organizations, and day-care settings.

There are good reasons for this. Time-Out is a humane, noninjurious type of punishment that can be administered and ended within a few minutes. And it tends to work well with a variety of young children.

I think it is effective because most parents believe in it, see its usefulness as a punishment, and come to trust themselves when using it. It works with children no doubt because young, active children don't like being confined to one spot—even for a few minutes.

That, of course, is what happens to a child during Time-Out. He or she is confined to a dull, nonstimulating place for a short period of time. By definition, Imposing Time-Out is taking a child away from reinforcement—some enjoyable activity such as playing—for a short period of time following disruptive or undesired behavior.

It doesn't matter too much where the Time-Out place is as long as it does not provide entertainment value for the child. Judi Perna complained because her four-year-old son Jerry enjoyed watching the other children play by looking out a window during Time-Out. Jean Morgan remembered that when she and her husband used Time-Out with their son Kurt, he fell asleep on his bed. Rita Carmichael told the group that when her daughter Amber was younger she could read a book or play a game during Time-Out.

These problems can be corrected easily. One of the quickest ways is not to use a child's bedroom for a Time-Out. Bedrooms of most children I know are anything but dull places. Better to choose a spot in the house where children have nothing to look at but a bare wall or corner. There is usually such a place in a dining room, formal living room, or hallway. Many parents designate a spot and a chair for Time-Out. That becomes the "Time-Out chair." Then, once a child understands what Time-Out is, the parent has only to say, "Go to Time-Out" for the child to go to the special spot.

It's also best to designate a period of time for this punishment. That is, when you tell a youngster to go to Time-Out, be sure also to specify how long the punishment will last: "You have to go to Time-Out for five minutes." Even though young children don't have a good grasp of time, at least this gives them an idea that the punishment will not last forever. Anxious or restless kids are liable to ask frequently, "Is it time yet?" With them it's helpful to use a timer, such as a kitchen timer, an alarm clock, an egg timer, or a specially made Time-Out clock (which some companies put out now for parents).

Setting a specific duration for Time-Out and using a timer are important because parents sometimes forget to watch the clock closely. If the youngster happens to be serving the Time-Out in silence, it's easy to relish the peace and let it drag on. But that isn't fair. When they get old enough to figure out that they are staying over their allotted time, children will start to question you about it. Also, it's good training for parents for the future when punishments may be longer (as when you restrict a teenager to the house for a week or limit the use of the phone for three days) and careful compliance with the duration can become an issue. So if it's important to stick to the designated duration of a punishment, it's also important to be fair and consistent.

How Long Should Children Be in Time-Out?

Parenting experts generally advise that children should be in Time-Out for about one minute for each year of age. That would mean a five-minute punishment for a five-year-old, a nine-minute Time-Out for a nine-year-old, and so on.

This guideline has two important benefits:

1. You are using a fair and moderate punishment that suits the developmental age of the child, and
2. You are not leaving the youngster in Time-Out too long.

When children are in Time-Out too long, not only do you run some of the risks of overly severe punishment that were mentioned earlier, but you add some new risks. Perhaps the most important one is that children will get bored, stop thinking about what they did wrong, and find more interesting ways to fill the time. Some children sing to themselves, lapse into daydreams or fantasies, or wander away from the Time-Out spot.

Researchers on children and adolescents are far from unanimous in their conclusions about what is the optimal duration of Time-Out. Some studies indicate that as little as a few seconds can be effective, and others say that longer Time-Outs (up to thirty minutes) are more likely to stop an undesired behavior. What this means for you as a parent is that you will have to experiment with various durations of Time-Out to find the most effective length of time for your child.

What if the Child Won't Go Willingly to Time-Out?

Many children refuse to go to Time-Out willingly. They dawdle, question the reason ("Why do I have to go to Time-Out?"), protest their innocence ("I didn't do anything wrong!"), blame someone else ("She hit me first"), or simply refuse ("No. I'm not going. You can't make me go!").

You can usually lead two- and three-year-olds to Time-Out by grasping their hand or taking a firm grip on their upper arm. Others can be picked up and plunked down on the Time-Out chair. However, children ages four, five, and older may be too big to be carried, and if they are determined to resist, they can make things very unpleasant for a parent. The youngster who is kicking, flailing, biting, and screaming often can't be led to Time-Out or picked up, at least not without some risk to the parent.

The next best approach is to announce that Time-Out doesn't begin until the child is sitting quietly in the Time-Out chair or place. Firmness is then needed: You do not allow the youngster to do anything else until the Time-Out is served. This is often difficult for mothers and fathers, especially Active Interveners, who tend to think that some direct action has to be taken immediately.

It becomes even more trying for parents when an active and persistent youngster not only refuses to go to Time-Out but runs away. The temptation, of course, is to chase the child and physically bring her back. Again, while this is possible for most physically active parents, it has a tendency to give attention to misbehaviors. In general, it is better to withhold attention from noncompliant behavior (in this case, running away, resistance, and refusal to go to Time-Out) than to get involved in chases and struggles to bring about compliance quickly. The alternative may take longer, but is best in the long run—even for impatient parents. Your practice with Ignoring will come in handy.

George and Becky Phillips consulted me about their five-year-old daughter, Bonnie, whom they described as "out of control." Bonnie was willful and defiant, and she refused to obey many reasonable requests. She cried frequently, hit her parents, and did not respond to their attempts at correction and punishment.

I told them that a good punishment for a five-year-old would be Time-Out. "Oh, we tried that," cried Becky. "It doesn't work at all because she refuses to stay in her chair."

I explained that while they thought they had tried it, I would like them to try it again, only this time following my rules. When Bonnie disobeyed a rule or failed to comply with an important request, she was to be told that she would have to spend five minutes in Time-Out. Furthermore, when she refused to go, she would be told that her punishment would not begin until she was seated quietly in the Time-Out chair. Also, both parents were to be there to support each other and to make sure that she could do nothing else until she served that five minutes.

"Oh, by the way," I said to them, "expect to spend a long time on this program of getting control this week. This will not be simple." I pointed out that often a child's behavior gets worse before it gets better when parents start using a punishment firmly.

One other point we covered was to combine Time-Out with Ignoring. They were not to respond to any of her efforts to avoid Time-Out other than to say, "When you are sitting quietly in Time-Out, your punishment begins."

I saw the Phillipses one week later. "What a week we had!" said George. "It started out awful," added Becky, "but it actually got better."

The first night after they left class, Bonnie's behavior was so intolerable that they told her she had to go to Time-Out. "No!" she said, and the battle was on. Both Becky and George were ready. They were willing, they said, to give up a night's sleep if they had to get Bonnie's behavior under control. It almost worked out that way.

"Do you know how long it took for Bonnie to serve her five minutes?" Becky asked with a dramatic pause before answering. "Six hours! Can you believe that?"

But Bonnie served her Time-Out. Two days later, she hit her brother and she was again told she had to go to Time-Out. That five-minute Time-Out was completed in under thirty minutes. Within seven days, her Time-Outs were being given and served in under twelve minutes. While this was still far from acceptable, it marked a turning point in the family. Becky and George were feeling more sure of themselves, and Bonnie's problems began to look less serious. Her parents felt they had more control over Bonnie once they knew how to use Time-Out effectively.

Say Little to Children During a Punishment

The less said during Time-Out the better. There is little reason for long speeches about the reason for the punishment, about how guilty you feel ("It hurts me that I have to do this to you"), or about how angry you are about the misbehavior ("Your behavior makes me so mad. I don't know what I'm going to do with you. I hope this teaches you a lesson, because nothing I've tried has worked").

If you need to say something, make it short, calm, and to the point, and remember the previous comments about Reprimands: "I do not like it when you hurt your brother. You are not allowed to push your little brother off the porch, as that could seriously hurt him. You must go to Time-Out for the next six minutes."

Questions or comments about fairness, the child's innocence, the length of time ("That's too long. How about four minutes?"), your qualities as a parent, or the "stupidity" of Time-Out as a punishment are to be ignored and not responded to. To repeat, you have one standard line to use: "Time-Out begins when you're seated quietly in the Time-Out chair." Say only that, and then strictly enforce it.

Another way of dealing with the misbehavior at the outset is to use a discipline technique called asking a Think Question. The purpose of a Think Question is to lead the youngster to tell you what she did wrong and why punishment is deserved. "Do you know why you have to go to Time-Out now?" you can ask.

If the child responds appropriately by saying something like "Yes, because I stepped on Janie's doll on purpose," you can say, "That's right. Whenever you destroy something that belongs to someone else you will be punished." If the child responds with an inappropriate or incorrect answer such as "I didn't do anything. Janie doesn't like her doll anyway," you can correct it: "You have to go to Time-Out because you destroyed something that belonged to someone else. That hurts their feelings and it's not fair." A Think Question can be used effectively before or after a punishment.

Teach Appropriate Behavior After Time-Out in Two Ways

After Time-Out is over, you can teach children why punishment was imposed by using Reasoning—simply giving a straightforward, brief reason for your action. For example, you might say after a Time-Out: "When you hit someone else, it is mean and cruel and hurts her feelings." By supplying the reason for the Time-Out you are making it clear to your child that the reason is not because you are mean, hostile, rejecting, or revengeful. There is usually a moral reason connected to a misbehavior that kids should be taught or may need to be reminded of. (For instance, hitting or causing pain to others is wrong; lying goes against what we believe in in this family; or stealing destroys the sense of trust we are striving for.) Using Think Questions and Reasoning are ways to teach more appropriate and desired behavior after a punishment.

Another way again involves discipline techniques discussed in previous chapters. After a Time-Out is over, the child should comply with any request or command that might have led to the punishment in the first place. Directing the child to comply gives you an opportunity to use Praise and Attention, Rewards and Privileges, and Reminder Praise.

Even if the child has just been allowed to return to previous activities or play, it is important to use the same positive techniques as soon as possible. This lets kids know that while some misbehaviors will be punished, correct and desired behaviors will be appreciated and reinforced.

After a youngster completes Time-Out for swearing at her father, she can be given Praise: "I heard you apologizing to Daddy. I really like to hear you speaking politely and asking for forgiveness. I'm proud of you."

Punishments often can't be avoided in raising children. But we can be sure that we're using the discipline techniques to bring about the behaviors we like and approve of more often than we use the punitive techniques. When we combine punishment with Praise and Attention, Rewards and Privileges, and Reminder Praise, we will be very effective with our discipline.

Summary

Punishment can be effective as long as it is carried out with appropriate:

- **Timing**
- **Severity**
- **Fairness**
- **Frequency**
- **Follow-through**
- **Context**

A Reprimand is a mild verbal punishment that allows parents to tell children the behavior that is disliked and disallowed. An effective Reprimand is one that is short and tells the child in definite terms what behavior or actions the parent doesn't like and doesn't want to see again. When combined with encouragement and directives for future behavior, along with moving closer to the child, maintaining direct eye contact, and using an authoritative voice, Reprimands can be successful punishments.

Time-Out is an effective, short punishment that has been found to reduce unwanted and disruptive behavior in both children and adolescents. It involves removing a child from a source of stimulation and reinforcement to an area that offers no such benefits. That usually means placing a child in a dull, nonstimulating area of the house for several minutes.

To increase the effectiveness of Time-Out:

- **Use Time-Out to stop more serious, undesirable, and dangerous misbehaviors.**
- **For the Time-Out area, select a spot that is dull and nonstimulating. This could be a corner, hallway, or stairway.**
- **Make only a brief statement (to cut down on potential reinforcing attention) when imposing Time-Out: "Since you did not come home when I called you, you will have to go to Time-Out for five minutes."**
- **Keep all parental attention to a minimum during the Time-Out period. Do not argue or provide rationales for the punishment or your actions. Ignore all temper tantrums, crying, protests, questions, and promises to behave during the Time-Out.**
- **Keep children in Time-Out for a relatively brief period of time. One rule of thumb is about one minute for every year of age.**
- **After Time-Out, the child must comply with any command or request that originally resulted in Time-Out.**
- **If the child resists going to the designated Time-Out chair or place, or leaves the area during Time-Out, say, "Time-Out begins (or continues) when you are seated quietly in Time-Out."**
- **Use Praise and Attention, Rewards and Privileges, or Reminder Praise when a child demonstrates positive, appropriate behavior following Time-Out.**

Homework Assignment for Week 6

Practice using Reprimands when it is appropriate to use a mild punishment. This might be after a misbehavior such as the breaking of a rule.

Following what misbehaviors did you use a Reprimand?

_____

_____

What did you say? Record exactly what you said during one or more Reprimands: ———————————————————

_____

_____

How did your child respond or act following each Reprimand? ———————————————————————

_____

_____

How did you feel about using the Reprimand?—————————

_____

_____

Decide which behavior you would like to discourage or eliminate through the use of Time-Out. Limit the choice to more serious or dangerous behavior; if you're concerned with actions that are merely annoying or irritating, consider using Ignoring to handle them. Write the behavior that requires the use of punishment here: ———————————————————————

_____

Each time the behavior you want to discourage occurs, respond with a Time-Out. There are a few other things to decide first:

Where will the Time-Out place be? Write the place that is dull and nonstimulating here: ————————————————

_____

How long will the child be in Time-Out? Write the length of time you believe is appropriate here (remember that one guideline is about a minute for each year of age): ——————————

_____

_____

What will you say when you assign Time-Out? Keep in mind that in general the less said the better. Write what you will say here: ———————————————————————

_____

How will you react if the child refuses to go to Time-Out?
Write your response here: ———————————————————————

———————————————————————————————————

———————————————————————————————————

Make a check mark on the lines for each day of this week
each time you use Time-Out:

MONDAY: ——————————————————————————

TUESDAY: —————————————————————————

WEDNESDAY: ————————————————————————

THURSDAY: —————————————————————————

FRIDAY:————————————————————————————

SATURDAY: ——————————————————————————

SUNDAY: ———————————————————————————

Answer the following questions after one week:

1. *Did the behavior I wanted to reduce or eliminate get*
   worse, as expected, before it began to get better? —————

   ———————————————————————————————

   ———————————————————————————————

2. *Did my child come to accept Time-Out as I used it consis-*
   tently? ————————————————————————————

   ———————————————————————————————

   ———————————————————————————————

3. *Did I find a duration of Time-Out that seemed to be best for*
   my child? ——————————————————————————

   ———————————————————————————————

4. *Did I make sure that I used positive discipline techniques*
   more often than I used Time-Out? ————————————

   ———————————————————————————————

10.

Week 7: Removing Rewards and Privileges to Eliminate Serious Misbehaviors

Y ou've been talking about punishments in here," a red-faced man blurted out toward the beginning of Week 7, "but I'm confused.

"We all know about physical abuse and all of that," he continued, "but how can you punish kids these days? All of this is blurry to me. You can't do anything these days, because your kid or a bleeding heart social worker will say it's abuse."

Several parents nodded their heads in agreement. "A Time-Out is okay with small children," a woman said, "but what are you going to do with a teenager? Aren't we just defenseless these days?"

Parents Are Often Confused About Punishment

As I've found in dozens of group meetings, parents are often confused about punishment in general and where the line is drawn between punishment and abuse in particular. It seems to many that if they can't use physical punishment, then the only choice is to let the child or teenager get away with unruly behavior. In other words, parents think they cannot enforce rules and behavior without strong-arm tactics.

But, of course, you can. There is a middle ground between helpless permissiveness that leads to young people doing whatever they wish, and the more punitive and potentially abusive use of physical punishment. Parents who are used to employing coercive methods, including spanking, feel especially powerless if they're told not to spank or use physical means of dealing with their children. There are, I'm happy to report, discipline techniques that can take the place of the risky physical methods of punishment. They can and do work even with young people who parents think are out of control.

Removing the Source of Pleasure from Kids

As indicated in the previous chapter ("Week 6: Effective Punishment to Discourage Problem Behaviors"), Time-Out means time away from a source of pleasure, stimulation, or fun. This is an effective punishment for most children. However, as they get older, many children see sitting in a Time-Out chair as something "babies" do—certainly not someone of the ripe old age of ten or twelve or older. They would prefer, if punishment is to be suffered, to endure one more fitting to their maturity.

There is research that shows that even with delinquent teenagers, Time-Out can be an effective punishment. With older children and teens, though, Time-Out should take a somewhat modified form.

One modified form of Time-Out is to send the teenager to his or her room rather than to a Time-Out chair or place. With sociable adolescents who like being around the family, in the family room, or where the action is, this tends to work fairly well if used infrequently. For teens who are more withdrawn, though, sending them to their room may not be an effective punishment.

But there is another punishment that usually works better for older kids and teens: Removing Rewards and Privileges. If Time-Out is removing the youngster from the source of reinforcement (being in the same room with a parent, sitting in the family room watching television, or playing outside on the swing set, for instance), Removing Rewards and Privileges is the opposite—taking away the source of enjoyment.

One of the reasons that this slightly altered punishment makes sense for older children is that while young children may dislike having their freedom of movement restricted, older children usually have learned to deal with the requirements of sitting still in various situations, such as at school where they must control any need for physical activity for an hour or more at a time. While they're gradually learning to suppress their need for physical movement over the years, their interests are shifting from physical play to friendships and independence from parental and adult supervision. For them, withdrawing or removing opportunities, activities, privileges, or tangible items becomes a more significant punishment.

Carmen Washington, mother of fifteen-year-old Benny, told about using this type of punishment with her son. "He brought home a computer printout of his grades last month," Carmen told her parent-training group, "and we were so pleased that he was doing better."

A few days later, the real computer report showed up in the mail from the school, and she discovered that Benny had manufactured the first printout on his friend's computer. She waited until her husband, Joe, came home and then called Benny at his friend's house and told him to come home. When he arrived, she and Joe confronted him.

"We're disgusted with your making up a false report card," said Carmen in the confrontation. "We thought we could trust you to tell us the truth, even if the truth wasn't pleasant."

"For falsifying your report card," said Joe in his deep, resonant voice, "you're grounded to this house for three weeks. That means no friends can come over, and you can't go over to Shannon's house."

Not only was Benny "busted"—as he later told his brother—but he was "grounded." Most teenagers have experienced being grounded, a form of Removing Rewards and Privileges.

Some Rewards and Privileges Parents May Remove as Punishment

Use of the telephone
Allowance
Television time
Use of bicycle
Playing with a video game
Staying overnight with a friend
Attending a party
Going to a special event
Playing with friends
Use of the family car

In psychological research, this kind of punishment is called "response cost," and has been found to be highly effective with misbehavior when used according to all the principles, outlined in the previous chapter, that make for effective punishment. What the term "response cost" means is that a child's misbehavior results in a cost to the child. He or she must pay a penalty by giving up a reward, opportunity, or activity.

The Reward or Privilege Removed Must Be Significant to Your Child

Whatever it costs the child or adolescent must be sufficient to make an impression. What is taken away or restricted must be meaningful and important to the young person. That, of course, suggests that you must know your child's likes and dislikes very well. Most young teenagers, for instance, live and die for talking to friends, so restricting the privilege of talking on the telephone is often a successful punishment.

Not every adolescent feels the same way, of course. Some don't have many friends, never invite someone over, or rarely use the phone. They might even be considered loners. If this sounds like your child, choose something that has greater meaning when a punishment is necessary.

Adolescents Become Adept at Manipulating Their Parents

That older children and teenagers are also more adept at manipulating parents must be kept in mind. It is typical for a teenager to say, "I don't care if I go to the dance or not. It doesn't bother me." Such claims can shake the confidence of some parents. If you have selected the activity or behavior rather carefully, then it doesn't matter what your child says. Such comments can be ignored or viewed as his or her way of getting in the last word or attempting to keep you from feeling that you've "won."

Furthermore, teenagers will try to bully you to relent and give in before the punishment is fully served, or set you up so that you don't use this punishment next time. For example, my daughter as a sixteen-year-old would try to talk me out of maintaining a restriction. "But, Dad," she would say, "I've got to go to the party. It's the most important one of the year. It's very, very important to me." By the time I had heard this line a few times, I began to conclude that everything she wanted to do couldn't be "very, very important" to her. Other young people I know use more bullying kinds of tactics, such as "If you ground me and make my life miserable, then I'm going to make your life miserable, too." Ignoring irritating comments or assertions is by far the best response.

What Is a Fair Punishment?

One of the hardest parts about punishing older children and teenagers is figuring out not only what is fair, but how long the punishment ought to last. The principles as given in the previous chapter hold true for Removing Rewards and Privileges as well as for Time-Out and other punishments. One principle was that punishment ought to be fair and moderate.

I remember a story that twenty-year-old Bart told me from his cell in a Michigan prison a few months ago. When he was about ten years old, he was caught shoplifting from a store. He didn't steal very often, and this was the first time he was caught.

When his mother found out about it, she was indignant. "If that's the way you're going to be," she literally screamed at him, "I'll show you what it will be like when you go to jail . . . because if you keep stealing, that's where you'll end up."

She went out that same day to a store and bought a padlock. She installed it on his bedroom door and locked him in his room. He could only leave to go to school and eat meals. This went on for more than two weeks before she figured he had learned his lesson.

The severity and the unfairness of his mother's response has lingered on in Bart's mind. He's not sure if her message ("you're going to end up in prison") shaped his life, but he did end up in prison.

Bart's mother didn't know much about punishment or about fairness. If she had responded in a less severe and fairer manner, she might have been able to teach Bart an important lesson. As it was, her overreaction taught him more about his mother than it did about his misbehavior.

How can we know what's fair and what's unfair when Removing Rewards and Privileges? With Time-Out, we have the guideline, mentioned in the last chapter, of one minute for every year of age. Unfortunately, there is no similar guideline to follow when using other punishments with teenagers. Parents have to rely on their judgment and, perhaps, some experimentation.

Our judgment, though, may not be an accurate guide, especially if we have been raised by parents who were overly harsh or too permissive. Judgment in discipline matters tends to be learned through our early childhood experiences with our own mothers and fathers.

A fair punishment is one that fits the actual offense. Locking a child in his or her room for two weeks is not fair for shoplifting, although requiring the child to stay there for a day could serve as an object lesson in what it "feels like to be locked up." Having the child go back to the store to return the stolen item, apologize to the store manager, and perhaps do some extra work at the store or at home is much more fair and relevant to the misbehavior.

Rita Carmichael asked the group whether her daughter's complaint about a punishment Rita had given was valid. Rita had taken away Amber's phone privileges for three weeks after Amber used the phone late at night without permission, and Amber said it wasn't a fair punishment. Pete Hernandez volunteered that Rita wasn't fair because her punishment lasted too long. "It would have been more fair if you'd said she couldn't use the phone the next night," Pete contended. "Three weeks is too long for a teenager to try to stay off the phone. Maybe it would actually encourage her to sneak the use of the telephone to call her friends." The rest of the group agreed.

In addition to the fairness of making the punishment proportionate to the misbehavior, there's an issue of practicality you should keep in mind: If you give a major punishment for a relatively minor misbehavior (which shoplifting tends to be for most youngsters), you will have little maneuvering room for imposing a more severe punishment if a more serious offense should occur.

For example, a while after Bart served his two-week "prison" term in his room, he began skipping school classes and became increasingly abusive toward his mother, eventually striking her. She ought to have had available a punishment for hitting her that was more severe than the one used for shoplifting. All she could escalate to beyond what she'd already done was either confining him to his room for a longer time or using physical punishment.

Bart didn't learn from her later punishments, which were, by the way, beatings with boards and canes, because he saw her as capricious, angry, and unfair.

Consistency Is Critical in Punishment

Along with fairness, there are other factors to consider in handing out this kind of punishment. One is consistency. Children and adolescents learn best when parental responses are consistent. In punishment, that means that if parents decide that a particular action—let's say coming home later than an agreed-upon curfew—rates a punishment in the form of Removing Rewards and Privileges, then every time the child comes in late, the child should be punished.

Consistency alone (assuming that the punishment is moderate and appropriate) will teach a great and lasting lesson. The lesson is: Whenever you come in later than your curfew, you will be in trouble and receive a punishment.

If consistency is as important as I believe it is, then the length and severity of the punishment assume less importance. While it should not be too mild or lax (say, losing the privilege of watching fifteen minutes of TV for coming home two hours late the night before), a moderate punishment (say, losing the use of the car for one day or one weekend) will dramatize the essential point—in this case, to persuade the teen to respect the curfew agreement.

Several Lessons Are Better than One

Consistency is important, but so is repetition. Having a lesson repeated can assist in the learning process. Many parents believe that if the misbehavior is repeated, the punishment didn't work.

Parents say something like this to me all the time: "I grounded her for a week for bringing the car home late and then she did it again. Obviously, she didn't learn from the punishment. This time she's grounded for a month."

There are two problems with this kind of response. For one thing, it assumes that young people always learn in one trial or one experience. It allows for no more than one mistake before justifying the conclusion that there is some deficiency in the young person's ability to learn from mistakes or in the particular punishment selected. It is a most unrealistic expectation in light of the tendency of most adults to make the same mistake more than once.

The other problem relates to the idea of increasing the intensity or duration of punishment. Many parents equate degree of severity with degree of effectiveness: The more severe the punishment, they think, the better young people will learn from it. Harsher punishments do sometimes work better than milder punishments, but I have seen better results from a different philosophy: The *certainty* of a negative consequence is more likely to teach a lesson than the *severity* of that consequence. This means that when a young person knows that a swift, equitable, but painful consequence will follow a misbehavior, he or she will learn that repeating the misbehavior makes no sense.

There's another booby trap in the notion that severity equals effectiveness. If a kid doesn't learn from one or two painful experiences, and is more likely to benefit from consistent experiences, then by increasing the length of the punishment (which is the usual way Removing Rewards and Privileges is made more severe), you reduce the number of opportunities to teach a lesson.

Let me give a practical example. Many parents are concerned about poor grades in school and try to teach children to be more highly motivated by restricting privileges (let's not argue the value of teaching motivation through punishment, although I suspect you can already guess where I stand on this issue). It is, for instance, a typical punishment to "ground" a kid to the house for a marking period to "improve your grades."

There are roughly four to six marking periods in a school year, depending on the school district. That means a parent would have four to six opportunities to teach a lesson through this type of punishment. Now, that's not many opportunities.

But if the school were to send home a weekly progress report, and the child had to face being grounded for one week at a time for poor performance, there would be about thirty-five opportunities during the school year to make a point. For my money, I'd put my bet on teaching a lesson with thirty-five opportunities rather than just six. When punishments are shorter, parents have more opportunities to teach a lesson.

Punishments of Long Duration Have Potential Negative Side Effects

In addition to reducing the number of opportunities to teach, punishments that go on too long may potentially go awry in other ways:

1. Kids may give up ("Using my bike wasn't that important anyway. I don't care if I never get it back").
2. Parents might forget when the restriction began and when it will end.
3. Parents sometimes feel guilty and give in ("All right, you can start having friends come over again").
4. Young people get frustrated and angry and decide to violate a rule anyway ("What difference does it make if I get grounded longer, I'm grounded all the time anyway").

Don't Use the Same Punishment All the Time

If you use the same exact punishment (taking away the use of the family car, restricting use of the telephone, confining a young person to the house or yard, or banning a favorite activity, for instance), you run a different kind of risk. That is that young people learn to live without the privilege—no matter what it is.

This is what I refer to as "settling in." Given almost any set of circumstances in life, people learn to adapt and settle in. I have seen many adolescents restricted to their house or their bedroom for months on end. After a while they come to accept it as part of their life and as a daily routine. Then the punishment has lost its effect.

What you want is for your child to work to remove the punishment or to wait anxiously for the punishment to end so he or she can return to the much-enjoyed activity or privilege. If the child settles in, then the old activity or privilege no longer has the value it once had, and that punishment is no longer effective.

Instead, keep every punishment you might use as a viable and effective option. The only way a punishment or the threat of a punishment will work is if your child fears it or wants to avoid it by doing the appropriate and approved behavior.

One way around this potential problem of diluting the effectiveness of a punishment through overuse is to vary your punishments. Do this in two ways: 1) Try to make each removal of a reward or privilege as fitting of the misbehavior as possible; and 2) vary what you remove, even for the same offense, especially if it's happening too often.

Sandra, the mother of two teenagers, wasn't sure if she had handled things right with fifteen-year-old Anthony. The incident started innocently enough, she explained to a group of parents during Week 7, when he was talking about getting his driver's license as soon as he turned sixteen.

Sandra told him that getting a driver's license was a privilege and would be contingent on his behavior being trustworthy at the time. As she tried to explain what she meant by responsible and trustworthy behavior, Anthony began to be more demanding and then became angry and sassy. At one point he swore at her.

"That will cost you," she said. "You're grounded to this house for two days."

"What!" Anthony retorted. "Screw you!"

"That's one more day," replied his mother evenly.

"You can't do that!" said Anthony. "It's not fair."

"Fair or not," said Sandra, "you're in this house for three days."

Anthony huffed out, shouting venomous remarks as he went to his room.

The next morning, Anthony left a note on the kitchen counter where his mother would see it before she went to work. "I'm sorry for the way I acted last night. I didn't really mean the things I said," he wrote.

"I'm not sure I did the right thing," Sandra appealed to the group. "Maybe I shouldn't have restricted him to the house, and maybe adding another day was just my way of getting even, and perhaps it wasn't necessary."

The parents in the group were supportive. "What I liked," said a woman who also had two teenagers, "was that you didn't really seem to lose your cool. I'm not sure I could have stayed in control the way you did."

"Yeah, and another thing," a second parent added, "was that it seemed to work. It's not very often our kids apologize to us. That's important to me."

I had to add my words of praise as well: "One of the things that I'm proud of you for is that you showed your disapproval of talking back and disrespect to you and backed it up with a punishment. There was nothing in my opinion wrong with that punishment. And you know what else? I think he wanted you to put some brakes on his behavior. That's why he apologized. Adding another day to the punishment gave him a firm message: Stop this now or you'll pay a bigger price."

Obviously, not every kid who talks back or even swears at you should be punished. But there are times when an important rule (in some families the rule might be that there will be no disrespect to parents) or the usual customs are violated. Parents need to show how much importance they put on rules, values, beliefs, or customs. A Punishment or a strong Reprimand is a way of doing this.

Vicky Amos told the group about her sixteen-year-old, Luis, who was in a juvenile detention center. He had done well there and had begun to have weekend passes home.

In his second month of weekends home, Vicky noticed that there were some slips in his previously gratifying record of improvement. At first there were little things—towels left on the floor of his bedroom, the bed unmade, some flip and sarcastic remarks to Vicky and her boyfriend.

"The biggest slip-up happened this last weekend when he was home," Vicky related to a number of parents sitting around a table. "He had a friend over on Saturday, and I was driving his friend back home on Saturday and Luis was with us in the car.

"I noticed that Luis had a bag with him on the floor in the front seat. So I asked what was in the bag.

"He said that he had some clothes in the bag because he was going to spend the night with his friend Ramone.

"I took my eyes off the road to stare at him, and I said to him, 'No, you're not. You did not ask for permission to do that. You're not going to start telling me what you're going to do.'

"Things got real quiet in the car," Vicky said. "Luis just looked straight ahead without saying anything."

Vicky dropped Ramone off and Luis returned with her. When they got home, Vicky thought something needed to be said to clear the air and let Luis know how the rules worked now.

"You are not going to come home and be the same Luis who was breaking the rules and getting into trouble," she told Luis. "When you don't ask me for permission to stay out with your friends, you will not be allowed to stay overnight. It's as simple as that. Not only can't you go to Ramone's this weekend, but not next weekend either. Next time remember to ask me first."

"Okay," said Luis, although Vicky wasn't sure that he was doing any thinking and may have just been seething under the surface of his stony expression.

Because Luis's aunt was coming for dinner that night, especially to see Luis, Vicky was going to be busy in the kitchen. "Luis," she asked, "would you mind watching your little sister while I work in the kitchen?"

Luis was still smarting from the incident in the car but he silently agreed. He actually played with his sister for an hour, and at one point Vicky could hear him reading a story to her.

After Vicky had the food under control, there was still about an hour before her sister was scheduled to arrive. Vicky was pleased about Luis's helping out and wanted to let him know this. "Luis, you've been real helpful with Celia," she said. "Would you like to see if your buddy down the street wants you to come over and play Nintendo for an hour or so? You did a great job with your sister."

"That's cool," said Luis. "I don't get much chance to play Nintendo in the Center."

"Well, you deserve it," said Vicky. "Be back in an hour."

"What I was thinking about after I let him go," said Vicky to the other parents, "was that maybe I was letting him off a punishment. He was grounded from spending a night at Ramone's, but should I have let him go to his friend's for an hour?"

Some of the other parents were puzzled, too. I tried to end some of the confusion. "You restricted Luis from spending an overnight with his friend. That was for not asking permission. Right?

"What does that have to do with complying with your request that he watch his sister?" I asked. Again, some parents were not sure.

I explained to the group the way I saw Vicky's handling of this situation. She did not ground him to the house forever. She did restrict him from overnights at Ramone's for two weekends. However, when he does some other appropriate and helpful behavior, like taking care of his sister, that must be reinforced. Vicky did that. And she didn't give up on his other punishment. That still stands. And it doesn't mean he won't do plenty of other things right. When he does, Vicky can still reward or praise those, even if letting him go to Ramone's in the next two weekends will not be a potential reward.

Kyle and Julia King told the group about their efforts to teach ten-year-old Leslie that finishing projects, especially homework, was important. She had a habit of failing to follow through, although she usually started out with good intentions.

The new rule of late was that Leslie was to spend one hour a night on her schoolwork. One afternoon, Kyle King called from work to say that a vendor had given him two tickets to the ice show in town, and he wanted to take Leslie, who was an ice skater herself.

"That would be lovely," said Julia. "You and she need to spend more time alone with each other. But, one problem. She needs to finish her schoolwork. You know we both agreed it was important that she get in the habit of devoting one hour a night no matter what."

"Okay," said Kyle. "How about getting her at it as soon as she gets home from school?"

"Agreed," said Julia.

Leslie was excited when she came home from school and heard the news. "Wow," she said. "Isn't that Kristi Yamaguchi in the show?"

"I think so," said her mother. "But the thing is, Leslie, you've got to have your schoolwork completed before you can go."

"No problem," said Leslie as she went to her bedroom to plan what to wear.

The next two times Julia checked on Leslie, she found her rummaging in her closet for a sweater and then talking on the phone to a girlfriend. "You've got to have your schoolwork done," reminded Julia.

"I know," said Leslie.

Kyle was late coming home and rushed in with the tickets in hand. "Is my girl ready for a night on the town?" he asked.

"I'm all set, Dad," said Leslie.

Julia was wearing a frown on her face, though. "There is a slight hitch in the plans," she announced. "Leslie agreed to get her schoolwork done early, but she's put it off and nothing is completed."

"Mom, you worry too much," said Leslie cheerfully. "I don't have that much, and I can get it done easily in the morning."

"That's not our agreement," said Julia.

"Aw, Mom," sighed Leslie, looking imploringly at her father.

"No, wait," interjected Kyle. "Your mother is right. We all agreed that your schoolwork was important and that you'd spend an hour a night at it no matter what. If you had time to do it this afternoon and you wasted the time, then you didn't live up to the agreement. Sorry, Leslie, no ice show for you tonight."

Leslie couldn't believe what she was hearing. "That's not fair," she sobbed. "This is very important to me. I told you I could do my work later tonight or tomorrow morning."

"That's not the way it works," said Julia. "When you don't finish your schoolwork, you forfeit the right to other privileges."

"Schoolwork is more important than an ice show," added Kyle. "There will be other shows. But living up to an agreement is more important."

In each of these three examples, the parents removed appropriate rewards and privileges. In each, also, they stood their ground despite the protests and the upset of their children. The punishments were relatively mild, and in each instance the young people learned valuable lessons about the importance of rules, values, and the firmness of their parents.

These three anecdotes, all true, are useful for one other reason. The parents did not expect that punishment would solve all their kids' problems. The removal of specific rewards and privileges was intended simply to deal with one problem. Other discipline techniques were being used by these parents to handle other problems and issues.

Summary

Removing Rewards and Privileges is a punishment that is an acceptable alternative to Time-Out and usually becomes more important as children grow older.

Removing Rewards and Privileges means withdrawing or taking away opportunities, privileges, desired activities, and tangible items as a punishment for a more serious or dangerous misbehavior.

Use this punishment during or immediately after a misbehavior. The rewards and privileges removed should be equivalent in value to the degree of the offense or misbehav-

ior. **Choose a reward, activity, or privilege that is meaningful to your child, and vary the use of this punishment so that the same item reward, privilege, or activity is not removed all the time.**

When you warn your child that he or she will lose a reward or privilege, make sure you follow through if the misbehavior occurs.

Do not remove a reward or privilege for too long. Moderate and consistent punishments are more effective than longer, more intense punishments.

After a punishment is over, make sure that you use discipline that reinforces positive and desired behaviors.

Homework Assignment for Week 7

Decide which behaviors you would punish by Removing Rewards and Privileges. Limit the choice to more serious or dangerous behaviors; if you're concerned with actions that are merely annoying and irritating, consider using Ignoring to deal with them. Write a behavior for which you will remove rewards and privileges this week here : ————————————————

————————————————————————————

————————————————————————————

Each time this behavior occurs, respond with Removing Rewards and Privileges. Here are some things you need to decide first:

What rewards, privileges, opportunities, or activities would you remove? Write those possible punishments here:————————

————————————————————————————

————————————————————————————

How long will the removal of rewards or privileges last? Write that here: ————————————————————————

————————————————————————————

————————————————————————————

Make a check mark on the line for each day of this week every time you remove a reward or privilege:

MONDAY: _____

TUESDAY: _____

WEDNESDAY: _____

THURSDAY: _____

FRIDAY: _____

SATURDAY: _____

SUNDAY: _____

11.

Week 8: Putting Discipline Techniques Together for a Better-Behaved Child

By Week 8 you should be seeing some positive results with your child. If your efforts have been diligent and consistent, you've probably enjoyed some of the same kinds of experiences that parents typically report during the eighth week of the program.

Judi Perna, the mother of three children, including four-year-old Jerry, admitted that before coming to the training class she had sometimes felt ready to "give my child away." Just before the eighth week, after Judi attended each class session and completed each homework assignment, the family took a short weekend vacation during which they stopped in a restaurant to have lunch.

"A woman came up to us," Judi related, "and told me how well-behaved Jerry was. I couldn't have been happier. But she should have seen how bad Jerry was just a few weeks ago."

Jean Morgan, whose son Kurt had had temper tantrums and always seemed angry before she and her husband Ron started the class, told about an incident that took place the week before.

"Kurt wanted to go swimming, and I knew he was overly stimulated and was getting grumpy," explained Jean. "To me that's always a signal that there's trouble ahead.

"I told him he had to go to his room for a while and settle down. I said that if he spent a half hour resting in his room, he could go swimming with his brother when he was finished. But if he didn't rest, there would be no swimming that day.

"I looked him square in the eye, ignored his protests, and really meant to back up what I said. He must have known that, because he went to his room, and when I went to check on him he was asleep. He got up in about an hour, was in a happy mood, and cheerfully went swimming with his brother.

"In the past," Jean said, "I would have argued with him and we both would have been mad. Also, he probably wouldn't have done what I wanted on top of it."

Ron Morgan noted another improvement: "We started taking away Kurt's Nintendo privileges for shorter periods of time, and it's working better. He's doing his chores and obeying me."

These kinds of stories become more frequent as the 8-week course proceeds. Parents try the discipline methods taught in the workshop and meet success.

But that doesn't mean that all problems are solved and you and your child go blithely off into the sunset without ever a cross word, angry exchange, misunderstood command, broken promise, ignored request, or misbehavior. Those will continue to happen. This program is not intended to turn you into Super Parent or your kids into wonderful role models for the rest of the children in the neighborhood. Rather, it is supposed to teach you how to effectively apply discipline techniques while increasing your self-confidence as a parent.

Expect to have a better-behaved child or adolescent, but also be realistic enough to know that you will need to continue to use the discipline techniques discussed in this book.

Week 8 is devoted to reviewing the 8 techniques and showing how to put all the discipline skills together to achieve the results you want with your child.

A Review of the Discipline Techniques

During each week of this course, at least one new discipline technique was introduced and discussed. While the purpose of studying several discipline skills is to have a variety of techniques to draw on, discussing them one at a time often doesn't give parents the bigger picture of how they all fit together. This week's lesson plan is to give an overview of the total course.

During Week 1, you learned about the 12 Keys to Effective Parenting. In Weeks 2, 3, and 4, you learned the following discipline skills:

Techniques to Increase Desired and Appropriate Behaviors

1. Praise and Attention
2. Rewards and Privileges
3. Reminder Praise

During Week 4, you also learned and practiced:

The 5-Step Method of Increasing Compliance

1. Identify the problem
2. State your expectation to your child
3. Have your child repeat back your expectation
4. State the consequences for compliance and for noncompliance with your expectation
5. Follow through in a consistent and firm manner

And during Weeks 5, 6, and 7 you added the following to your parental repertoire:

Discipline Skills to Discourage Undesired and Inappropriate Behaviors

1. Ignore Behavior
2. Reprimand Misbehaviors
3. Impose Time-Out
4. Remove Rewards and Privileges

In the 8 weeks, then, you learned 8 distinct discipline skills that can be applied to a variety of behaviors with which you may be confronted. Far from being powerless, you are now well-equipped to handle most behavioral challenges.

The 8 Steps to a Better-Behaved Child

In addition to the discipline techniques, we can look back at the 8 class sessions in another way. Each of the sessions in the course can be considered a step in a process of developing better behavior in your child. Here are the 8 steps toward a better-behaved child:

Step 1: Monitor your critical and negative remarks; make sure you are not giving too much attention to misbehaviors.

Step 2: Begin using Praise and positive Attention to reinforce the behavior you would like to see happening more often.

Step 3: Give Rewards and Privileges to reinforce more desired and appropriate behavior. Use this skill especially with behaviors that are not currently occurring or do not take place often enough.

Step 4: Add Reminder Praise as another way of reinforcing desired behavior.

Step 5: Use the 5-Step Method of Increasing Compliance by clearly stating your expectations and giving positive consequences for compliance and negative consequences for noncompliance.

Step 6: Begin to systematically ignore minor, irritating, and attention-getting misbehavior.

Step 7: Use punishments—Reprimands, Time-Out, or Removing Rewards and Privileges—to discourage unwanted and inappropriate behavior.

Step 8: Put all of the discipline techniques together to respond effectively to difficult and unwanted behavior.

Putting Them All Together

I have made only occasional suggestions up to this point about how to use the discipline skills you've learned in a coordinated fashion. It's time to go into more detail about this. To do so I'll use some examples from families who went through the 8-week parenting program.

Eight-year-old Robbie was shopping with his mother in the grocery store. He didn't really want to be there and obviously preferred to be playing outside or going for the ice cream he'd been promised after the grocery shopping was completed. To show his unhappiness, he was demanding ("Hurry up! Let's go!"), impatient ("Why are you reading the cans? Just get them and let's go!"), and somewhat obnoxious.

When his mother seemed to be spending too much time at the deli counter, Robbie's impatience became overwhelming for him. He grabbed a spaghetti sauce display rack and began shaking it, saying, "When are we going to get out of this stupid store?"

His mother shot a glance in his direction and instantly envisioned what could happen next if he pulled too hard on the rack of glass jars filled with red sauce.

Since his mother had just finished the 8-week parenting program and had learned how to use the discipline techniques discussed in this book, she reacted differently from the way another parent might. Calmly, she took a few quick steps to where Robbie was standing and spoke quietly but firmly to him.

"Robbie, come over by the counter and help me make the selection for dinner tonight," she said. "If you help me, I think we can finish our shopping quicker, don't you?"

Because she stared directly at him and was bent down to his level, he saw that she meant business. He also heard what she was saying to him. In effect, her message was, "If you're frustrated and impatient, then help me and you get out of here faster."

But things didn't end there. His mother was aware that she had done little in her haste that morning to prepare him for the shopping trip, and she realized it was still not too late to do so. As they got the last container from the deli clerk, she led Robbie down a deserted aisle and stopped the cart. Getting down to his level and taking him by the shoulders, she said, "Robbie, I know this is not what you want to be doing this morning, but we have to get our shopping chores out of the way. The best way for this to happen is for you to help me. You will be a big help if you push the cart while I pick out what we want.

"I expect you to push the cart slowly and to help me look for the food I want to buy. If you do this, then we'll get out of here faster and we'll have time to get the ice cream you wanted. Understand? Okay, repeat back to me what I just said."

Robbie had trouble keeping his eyes focused on his mother while she was talking. He glanced away and then back to her. She still had her hands on his shoulders and he tried to twist away.

"First," she said, "just tell me what it is I expect of you."

"Let me go!" said Robbie.

"No. First, tell me what I want from you," said his mother forcefully but without anger.

"All right," said Robbie. "You want me to push the cart and stay with you and not yell at you."

"That's right!" his mother said. "Very good. Now, what will happen if you do all of that?"

"We'll get to stop for ice cream."

"Right," she said. "So let's get at it, because I'm hungry for some strawberry ice cream, too."

Robbie, now thinking about what was coming when they were finished, said "Mmm" and reached for the handle of the shopping cart.

As they went down each aisle, his mother called out two or three items for him to look for in the aisle. When he spotted something they needed, she used Praise and Attention: "Sharp eyes! You found those so fast!"

Another time she commented on how quickly they were progressing with his help.

Later, when they were enjoying ice cream sundaes with their groceries packed in the trunk of their car, she took the opportunity to thank him for all of his help. She didn't ever mention the spaghetti sauce near-disaster or his "bad attitude" at the beginning.

If this were a test of what you've learned so far, you could probably pick out several discipline techniques Robbie's mother used in this sequence of events. In the space of a few minutes, she used the 5-Step Method, Praise and Attention, and Rewards and Privileges. She handled them in a patient and calm way. She could have used even more discipline skills and clearly would have if what she tried hadn't worked.

Ten-year-old Sarah Reynolds had a problem that had gone on for nearly eight years. It constantly frustrated and befuddled her parents, who said that they had tried everything they knew about discipline to bring about change.

The problem was this: Sarah woke up in the middle of each night and came into her parents' room. No matter what they tried, they couldn't break their daughter's habit. Taking her back to her bedroom several times a night, locking her door, making threats, spanking her, rewarding her, reasoning with her, and making promises all proved to be ineffective. When Sarah was denied access to her parents' room, she'd start crying, then escalate to a temper tantrum, and eventually end up vomiting. Usually, out of frustration, exhaustion, and need for sleep, her parents would give in and let Sarah sleep on a blanket on the floor in their bedroom.

Karen and Dwayne Reynolds decided to put to use some of the things they learned in the 8-week parenting program to try to change this most annoying and persistent problem.

They started with a very clear statement about their expectations, one that left no uncertainty about their wishes. Together, both parents had a talk with Sarah one Sunday afternoon when they had just finished a family bike ride.

"You know the bedtime problem?" Karen began. "Well, we have a few things to say about that. Your father and I have been thinking a lot about it and talking about what to do. We want you to know exactly what we expect of you now that you're ten years old."

"Right," echoed Dwayne, picking up where his wife left off.

"We have some expectations, and we want you to know just what they are. The major expectation is that you sleep the whole night, every night, in your own bed in your room."

"Yes," said Karen. "We've fought too much about you coming into our room, and we don't want this type of problem any more. You get too upset about us trying to keep you in your room just as we get too mad at you."

"Not only do we expect you to sleep in your own bed every night," repeated Dwayne, "but we expect that there will be no more tantrums about this. But to help you, we promise that if you sleep in your own bed at night, you will be allowed to watch television the next day and you will get an allowance of three dollars and fifty cents a week."

"If you don't sleep in your bed for the whole night," added Karen, "you will get no television the next day, and fifty cents for that day will be deducted from your allowance.

"Now, just to make sure you understand this, we want you to repeat back to us what we expect of you. Okay?"

"Okay," said Sarah, who hadn't said anything up to this point. "You want me to sleep in my own bed at night."

"Right," said her mother. "And if you do, what happens?"

"I get to watch TV and get an allowance."

"Okay," said her father. "What if you leave your room or come into ours and go to sleep?"

"I lose my allowance and can't watch TV," said Sarah.

"Well, not exactly," corrected Karen. "You only lose fifty cents of your allowance every day."

"Can't I watch any TV?" inquired Sarah.

"Nope, sorry," said her father. "Sleep in your own bed and watch TV. Sleep in our room and lose all TV."

"But that isn't fair," protested Sarah.

"Maybe not," said her mother, "but that's what we decided."

"We're going to stick to it, too," said her father.

That night, her parents reminded Sarah about the expectations and consequences as she was being tucked in and before she said her prayers.

But as her parents anticipated, it was not going to be easy for Sarah to change. They had agreed on taking turns to be awake and ready to deal with Sarah. It was her mother's turn the first night, and she was prepared to deal with Sarah when she woke up at about 2:00 A.M., which was her usual routine.

When Sarah came into her parents' room dragging a blanket and started to curl up on the floor, Karen leaped out of bed quietly. Taking Sarah by the arm, she said firmly, "Back to your own room." She then led her down the hall to her room.

"I'm scared in my room," Sarah said. "I can't go back to sleep."

Karen said nothing, and in fact didn't even look at Sarah.

"Mommy," said Sarah with more desperation in her voice. "Please. Don't make me go back into my room. It's too scary. Just let me sleep in your room tonight. Please. I promise this will be the last night. Please!"

"No," was all Karen said. She took Sarah to her bed and tucked her in. "You will be able to sleep better here," she said. Then she left the room, just as she had at 9:00 P.M. when Sarah had first gone to bed.

Before Karen was back in her room, she heard Sarah's slippers shuffling down the hall behind her and the sniffles that always came before the more intense crying of a temper tantrum.

Turning around, she silently advanced toward Sarah. Sarah threw her arms around her mother and hugged her tightly. "Mommy, I love you," she said. "I want to be close to you. Don't make me stay in my room. Please!"

With the ten-year-old girl attached to her waist, Karen returned to Sarah's room without responding with her usual "I love you, too." Sarah's crying was becoming louder with every step back to her room. Inside the room, Karen maneuvered Sarah back into bed. "I expect you to stay in your bed," she said in a controlled manner.

As she stepped out of the door of Sarah's bedroom this time, she closed the door completely and held onto the handle.

Within seconds, Sarah was pulling on the door and beginning to cry louder.

"Let me out!" Sarah demanded. "I have to go to the bathroom. . . . I'm going to throw up. I'm getting sick."

Karen said nothing. She held tightly to the door handle as Sarah continued to struggle to pull the door open. After five minutes, Karen let go of the handle. A crying Sarah came out of the room. Without letting her get a full step out of the room, her mother guided her back in and to her bed.

"Don't go, Mommy," Sarah implored. "Please stay with me until I go to sleep. I'm too afraid without you."

"It's important for you to learn to return to sleep without me," said Karen. "You can learn to do this."

It went like this for some two hours before Sarah fell asleep on the floor by her door. But she didn't sleep in her parents' room, and her fatigued mother finally was able to collapse in her own bed.

The next morning, Dwayne went to work early, and before Karen went to her job she talked to Sarah. "You slept in your room all night and I'm proud of you for being able to do that. You will be able to watch television today, and here is fifty cents of your allowance.

"Tonight, we will expect you to stay in your own room and to sleep there. The consequences we talked about are still in effect. All right?"

"Okay," said Sarah, smiling as she was handed fifty cents.

The next night, and for many nights that followed one or the other of her parents were "on duty" to make sure Sarah was returned to her room and not allowed to sleep anywhere except in her own room. For Sarah there was much crying and some vomiting; for her parents, more than a little anxiety and insecurity. Yet they stuck faithfully to the regime. Even when it wasn't voluntary, if Sarah ended up sleeping anywhere other than in her parents' bedroom, she got her allowance and the privilege of watching TV.

As the nights went on, they attempted to increase the

length of time they would wait before responding to her crying. They also increased the length of time they held onto the door when she tried to leave after the second or third time she was returned to her room.

On more than one occasion after one of her parents thought that she was asleep in her room and they had gone to sleep in their own bed, they were surprised the next morning to find Sarah rolled up in a blanket on their floor. They made sure that she got no allowance on those days, and no TV either.

How long did it take before they began to see signs of a positive change? It was nearly six weeks of lost sleep and constant nighttime alertness before Sarah slept the whole night in her own room without leaving once.

That next day, Karen and Dwayne Reynolds were ecstatic, and let Sarah know by giving her some "extra" rewards. Dwayne brought home a new doll for Sarah's doll collection, and Karen fixed her favorite dessert for dinner. They both said how pleased they were with how well she was doing.

Things didn't miraculously change after that. The very next night, Sarah got up and returned to her parents' room. They were ready for it and went through previous routines. But gradually the situation improved.

By sticking to what they said and by being very consistent with both reinforcements and punishments, Sarah's parents conveyed the message that they meant business. Sarah slowly came to understand that if she wanted an allowance and the privilege of watching TV, she had to change her behavior and the habits she'd acquired over eight years.

Within four months, Sarah was sleeping the night through in her own bed at least four nights a week. Her parents found that she tended to slip back into old patterns when there were other upsets or changes in her life. That helped them to understand that changes and adaptations were traumatic for Sarah. She didn't make transitions well at all. Until this new pattern of sleeping the whole night in her own bed was well established, Sarah was not allowed to spend the night with her cousin or her grandparents. She was told that when she slept every night in her own room, she could begin spending overnights away from home—but only if everyone agreed that there would be no change in the routine or expectations when Sarah was away from home. Grandparents and aunts could not disrupt the new bedtime ritual and schedule.

As you can tell, the Reynolds called upon every discipline technique they had learned in order to deal with a deeply ingrained pattern of behavior. This sleep pattern had been established eight years earlier and reinforced, in one way or another, thousands of times. To change it required resolve and consistency on the part of Karen and Dwayne. Because they were strong enough to provide that resolve and consistency, and because they could integrate all the steps and discipline techniques they'd learned, they were able to help Sarah to change her behavior.

The Use of Discipline Techniques With Other Troublesome Behaviors

Parents usually bring up several other problem behaviors in the final session of the program and seek guidance on how to put the skills together to handle specific problems effectively. The following examples are among the typical concerns that arise in the final session:

• *The child who can't seem to remember to ride on the sidewalk and stay out of a dangerous street.* Often this is a four- or five-year-old, although older children may have this problem as well.

The human tendency of parents is to yell, nag, remind, and threaten. But I suggest the most effective way to handle this kind of problem is to resolve to stay outdoors with your youngster during bike riding for as long as it takes to establish that you mean it when you state your expectations (e.g., "I expect you to ride only on the sidewalk. I do not want you riding your bike in the street").

Then add Praise and Attention and usually Rewards and Privileges (for instance, continuing to allow the child to bicycle ride on that day) for compliant behavior, and punishment for noncompliant behavior. A negative consequence could be that every time the child rides in the street, the child must put the bike down and sit on a chair on the porch for five minutes. For you that means that every time the child rides into the street, you stop, put the bike away for a few minutes, and send the child to a Time-Out chair on the porch. Once the Time-Out period is over, you return the bike and allow the child to use it. Until your child has learned to avoid riding in the street and until you can trust that he or she will stay on the sidewalk, the child must not bike ride unless a parent is supervising.

• *The child or teenager who doesn't seem to have any motivation to excel at school.* Parents are frequently perplexed by this problem, which may go on for several years and becomes more critical when children enter junior high and high school. To make a change requires a careful examination of the possible reasons for the problem and the structuring of a parental approach combining a number of discipline techniques.

While a lack of motivation in school can be caused by such problems as low intelligence, hyperactivity, or learning disabilities, if these factors have been ruled out, then the approach might be as follows:

1. Start by devising a routine for study and homework. It should include a suitable study place in the house, a definite time to study each day, and a way to make sure the study materials get home each day.
2. Let your child know your expectations related to studying, doing homework, and bringing home correct assignments and materials each day.
3. State the consequences of compliance and noncompliance with your expectations.
4. Use Praise and Attention as well as Rewards and Privileges when your child makes efforts to study more and spends time at homework.

5. Follow through with setting limits (meaning the child knows not only what is expected but also what the rules and boundaries will be; for instance, "no other activities are allowed during the designated study period") and imposing punishment when your expectations for study are not met. Respond to failure to live up to your expectations by Removing Rewards and Privileges.

6. Use Ignoring Behavior to respond to most complaints and protests regarding the routine.

7. Consistently work at using Praise and Attention and Rewards and Privileges to improve study habits; avoid scoldings and nagging. However, when necessary, use punishment to reinforce clear expectations.

• *Young people who talk back or are disrespectful to you as their parent.* This is a common problem in our society. It may have a lot to do with generations of growing disrespect toward authority figures in general, as well as the breakdown in family structure. Fueling this disrespect are any number of movies that cater to the humor value in disrespect to authority. Of course, as our penchant for finding the foibles of authority figures continues, we are never disappointed to learn that people in positions of authority have clay feet and often don't deserve our respect.

Add to these reasons parental confusion about allowing kids to express their feelings, and we often have what constitutes a mixed-up society breeding young people who believe they have a right to say anything to adults.

The first part of dealing with this problem is to get your values straight and to make sure you model appropriate, respectful behavior to your children and others. Then, establish a few basic rules for your children. One suitable rule might be: Children will treat people, including family members, with respect. Again, as with other misbehavior, begin by stating your expectation to your child: "I expect that you will treat your father and me with respect. You can express your opinion, and you're entitled to your feelings. However, when you go beyond simply expressing your opinions and are disrespectful, then we will be very unhappy with you and there will be negative consequences."

Let your child know what the consequences will be. "When you consistently treat us with respect, then you will be allowed privileges like having friends over and going places you want to go."

Also specify the negative consequences. "When you talk back or talk to us in a disrespectful manner, then you will lose privileges to go out or to be with your friends."

Once you have stated your expectations, be prepared to give immediate feedback in the future. When your child talks to you in an appropriate way, say so: "I'm proud of you for the way you handled it when I told you that you couldn't go to the concert. You let me know what you think without attacking me or yelling. I like that."

Similarly, if your child slips and is disrespectful, say that immediately as well. Do this in a forceful, but not angry or disrespectful, manner: "That's disrespect. I told you that we will not tolerate your talking to us like that any more. Because of that, you won't be going out to the basketball game with your friends tonight."

Ignore arguments and attempts to talk you out of punishments. Follow these guidelines explicitly and attempt to use Praise and Attention as well as Rewards and Privileges much more frequently than you are using Reprimands and other punishment.

The three examples just discussed not only demonstrate how to deal with some of the questions and difficulties parents raise in the last session of the program, but also illustrate that the discipline techniques taught in this book can be applied to a variety of situations. By combining the 8 steps outlined earlier in this chapter, you can handle almost any behavior problem you might have with a child or teenager.

Summary

You can put together all the discipline techniques taught in this book to deal with misbehavior or inappropriate behavior from your child when it occurs.

These discipline techniques are:

A. Discipline Techniques to Increase Desired and Appropriate Behaviors
 1. Praise and Attention
 2. Rewards and Privileges
 3. Reminder Praise
B. The 5-Step Method of Increasing Compliance
 1. Identify the problem
 2. State your expectation clearly
 3. Ask the child to repeat back your expectation
 4. State the consequences for compliance and for noncompliance
 5. Follow through in a consistent and firm manner
C. Discipline Techniques to Discourage Undesired and Inappropriate Behaviors
 1. Ignore Behavior
 2. Use Reprimands
 3. Impose Time-Out
 4. Remove Rewards and Privileges

Use all of these discipline skills and techniques in a coordinated fashion to bring about the behavior you want and to stop the behavior you don't want.

Part III

Beyond 8 Weeks: Advanced Discipline and Maintenance for Managing Behavior

12.

What If Your Child Isn't Better

Behaved?

L et's say that you have read this book carefully up to this point, and that you have faithfully completed each homework assignment. But try as you might, although you've noticed some changes (perhaps especially in your own reactions), you don't see sufficient improvement in your child or adolescent.

He or she may still be difficult to live with, acting up or acting out, and too angry too often. Maybe your child is getting into trouble even though you believe you're handling discipline fairly well. So, what do you do now?

That's what this and the next chapter ("Using ESCAPE to Handle Out-of-Control Children") are about. They explore other ways to deal with kids' difficult behavior. You might call the techniques in these two chapters Advanced Discipline. The preceding chapters presented a program of basic discipline that has proven to be effective when followed conscientiously. But sometimes problems are so difficult or so deeply ingrained in a child's (or family's) way of thinking and behaving that no amount of change in the discipline methods of choice will bring about significant changes in behavior.

There could be other reasons why the discipline techniques and procedures so far discussed haven't produced a significant result. One possibility is that your youngster's behavior is too far along the path to delinquency. That is, maybe the acting-out behavior includes breaking the law. Because such behavior frequently has its own set of payoffs (for instance, stealing results in loot being acquired; certain kinds of delinquent actions bring status from peer groups or criminal adults; drug use results in a "high"; and so forth), using the basic discipline techniques may not result in a change in the delinquent acting-out behaviors.

Another possibility may be that the young person is too angry, hostile, or resentful to respond successfully to a change in parental behavior or a change in parental methods of discipline.

Finally, a child in a family environment in which there is too much arguing and too little communication will not change quickly or easily. Not only does such a climate breed intense anger and hostility, but it is almost impossible to communicate effectively in such a household.

If you face any of these situations, should you give up?

Certainly not. Just recognize that the discipline techniques discussed in previous chapters and your valiant efforts haven't brought about desired results. Now it's time to do something different.

Don't, however, stop using the techniques you learned in the 8-week program. Those are invaluable and vital skills, and they are essential in the long run to making family life and relationships work. Instead, add something new to your repertoire. Like contracting.

What Is Contracting?

Contracting is a way of mediating family conflicts and negotiating a settlement of tough family problems. It's a way of putting on paper obligations, agreements, and expectations of behavior to help reduce arguments and misbehavior. It's a method for devising a plan for behavior change.

In general terms, a contract addresses family disagreements, starts a process of communication, and settles issues of rewards and privileges all in one package. Contracts have been found to be useful in changing more serious childhood or adolescent behavior problems that have not responded to other methods or approaches.

In practical terms, a contract is a written agreement that says who is to do what, to whom, under what circumstances, and with what consequences.

The Assumptions Underlying Contracts

There are four important assumptions that underlie the successful use of contracts.

Assumption 1: Parents often are not consistent or effective in their approach to using Rewards and Privileges with their children. By straightening out how parents administer the giving of Rewards and Privileges, they can successfully change some difficult behavior problems.

Assumption 2: The parents have tried setting up obligations and rules governing how children are to be given Rewards and Privileges within the family context. The misbehavior shown by young people, however, usually means they are not living up to their obligations within the family. Contracts help to focus discussion on those obligations and show in a very direct way that when young people meet their duties and obligations, they begin to have Rewards and Privileges.

Assumption 3: When the obligations and rules are spelled out on paper, and when it is clear how children can earn Privileges and Rewards by meeting their responsibilities, the process of how a functional family operates becomes wonderfully lucid for all members of the family.

Assumption 4: When families have openly negotiated a contract and signed it voluntarily, they are likely to live up to the terms of that agreement. Most young people and adults with whom I've worked over the years will live up to an agreement when they have been part of the process and feel they haven't been coerced into making the agreement or signing a document.

A Family in Need of a Contract

The Walterses were a good example of a family that needed a contract.

Composed of a father, a stepmother, and an adolescent son, the Walters family had had problems in communication for several years. The initial communication difficulties led to fifteen-year-old Jeff becoming increasingly angry, resentful, defiant, argumentative, and disobedient.

Problems began almost simultaneously with his father David's remarriage when Jeff was thirteen and facing the onset of adolescence. At first Jeff liked the idea of having Beverly as his stepmother, but later he started acting angry and resentful toward her. Eventually, this became more generalized behavior directed at both Beverly and David.

Jeff stopped doing his chores, spent more time away from home with friends, and found a new group of friends who had school problems and less supervision at home. He stayed out too late, came home drunk more than once, and threatened to run away if he couldn't stay out later.

His grades also began to slip, and by the tenth grade he had begun to get into trouble at school by cutting classes, disrupting his classes when he was there, and failing to complete schoolwork. His parents complained that he lied about his schoolwork, and there were arguments about school, his chores, and the rules at home.

Jeff's father and stepmother were very concerned about Jeff's changed attitude and behavior. They tried to talk to him many times. On each occasion, though, the discussion didn't seem to get anywhere, and more often than not they became frustrated and angry or just felt like giving up. Jeff, too, got very frustrated and angry. He expressed his anger verbally by attacking his parents, accusing them of being too rigid and restrictive, and calling them names.

More than once, they tried using rewards to bring about the behavior they wanted. At first Jeff responded with enthusiasm and made some efforts, but the changes didn't last very long. Then, they tried a contract.

The contract was the idea of David and Beverly, and the first one they wrote read:

CONTRACT

Jeff will do the following:

1. *Come home on time.*
2. *Never drink alcohol.*
3. *Always treat his parents with respect.*
4. *Attend school every day without missing any classes.*

I, Jeff Walters, agree to live up to this contract.
Signed: Jeff Walters
Signed: David Walters
Signed: Beverly Walters

Jeff's parents told him to read it over and sign it. He signed, although later he admitted that he did so only because he was afraid of being grounded to the house "for six months" if he refused.

While Beverly and David knew that something different had to be attempted to begin the change process, their first effort at a contract was a failure. Like the previous use of rewards, the contract was helpful for a few days. When Jeff didn't live up to its provisions, however, the parents didn't know what to do.

A Better Contract

The Walters family had made a start, albeit a poor one. But their first contract was a good place to begin—by throwing it out and starting over.

That, of course, suited Jeff just fine. However, he was skeptical when his parents told him they wanted to talk about and negotiate a "real" contract between parents and kids—not just shove something in front of him and tell him to sign it.

The first step was to bring the family together and talk about what each wanted from the other. This is where all contract negotiations must begin. The many frustrating and upsetting things that are happening in the home must be addressed. Getting grievances out in the open for discussion is essential. That might not occur in a first or second meeting. If coercion has been used with a youngster before, he or she may well be dubious about being told to feel free to propose anything to put in a contract. But that's what has to happen.

Jeff Walters had complaints about not being allowed to stay out late enough, and he didn't like the way Beverly, a relatively new stepmother in his life, took on discipline responsibilities. But it took three meetings before he said he didn't like his father's anger or the way his father didn't stick up for him in front of Beverly.

Of course, parents have their desires and complaints, too. David wanted Jeff to do his chores, to hang around with "decent" kids, and to get above-average grades. Beverly wanted Jeff to treat her with respect, to do his own laundry, and to stay away from alcohol.

As these ideas, desires, and complaints were brought out into the open, a first draft of a new contract began to take shape. The first draft looked like this:

CONTRACT DRAFT

Effective dates: December 15 to January 15
We, the undersigned, agree to the following terms:

If Jeff comes home on time,
> *Then his parents will let him stay out until 11:30 P.M. one night each weekend.*

If Jeff does his own laundry,
> *Then Beverly will iron his school clothes.*

If Jeff completes his homework each night (Sunday–Thursday),
> *Then his parents will give him an allowance of $10.00 a week.*

If Jeff talks to both parents with respect,
> *Then his parents will allow him to have any friends come over without making critical remarks.*

Bonus: If Jeff achieves all A and B grades on his report card, his parents will give him a bonus of $25.00 which he can spend in whatever way he chooses.
Penalty: For every class Jeff cuts, he will forfeit one dollar ($1.00) from his allowance.
If Mr. Walters gets angry at Jeff, Jeff gets an extra dollar ($1.00) added to his allowance that week.

Revising the Contract

Usually there are problems with the first draft of a contract. For one thing, favorite issues may not be properly addressed. For another, it may become apparent that some clauses in the contract do not work, are poorly spelled out, or are unenforceable. This was certainly true with the Walters' contract.

"What does it mean 'come home on time'?" questioned Jeff during a meeting to discuss the first draft of the contract.

David tried to explain: "That means coming home at the time we agree upon any time you go out," he said.

"Yeah," responded Jeff, "but what if I go out when you're not here and nothing is said about what time I'm supposed to come home?"

"Good point," agreed Beverly. "Why don't we just come up with a time now for any time Jeff goes out, and then there won't be any question about it?"

"I don't know," said Jeff. "You'll probably say I have to be in at seven o'clock or something."

"Well, remember," added his father, "we're discussing everything, and you don't have to agree with anything unless you want to."

"So, I can say midnight on school nights?" said Jeff.

"You can say that," said Beverly, "but we have to agree, too."

"We need to come up with times that are fair," suggested David.

"I think ten o'clock is fair on school nights," ventured Jeff.

"Ha!" said David. "This is the kid who's doing so well in school he doesn't have to worry about homework."

"Let's not get sarcastic," cautioned Beverly. "I think ten o'clock is too late on school nights. But eight o'clock is fair."

"Well, I don't think so," responded Jeff. "No one else has to be home that early."

"Well, then," said David, "how about nine o'clock if you have your homework done first? Could you live with that?"

"Yeah, I guess," said Jeff. "But I wanted to ask about this homework part in the contract. What if I don't have homework?"

"What do you mean?" asked his stepmother.

"I mean what if I don't have homework that night and you don't believe me?"

"That is a problem," his father agreed. "How can we know that you're telling the truth? You've lied to us before about homework."

"You never believe me," interjected Jeff, getting defensive.

"We'd believe you if you told the truth," said Beverly, showing traces of anger.

"Don't call me a liar!" said Jeff.

"Wait a minute," said David, trying to calm things. "I think we both want to believe you. If you tell us the truth, we will. How can we be sure that you don't have homework?"

"I don't want to bring home any stupid weekly progress reports like last year," said Jeff.

"Okay," said Beverly. "I've got it. How about this. We'll let you have the benefit of the doubt. We'll trust you if you say you have no homework. However, if you are trying to snow us, we'll know at the end of the marking period by your grades. We've already agreed that you get a bonus of twenty-five dollars for good grades. If you get lower grades and if the report card shows that you're not completing homework, then we change the contract and you have to bring home a weekly progress report. So it's really up to you."

"So I don't have to bring home a weekly progress report. Just if I screw up?" asked Jeff.

"Right," said David. "Just if you aren't doing your homework and hiding this from us."

There were other questions all three members of the family raised. After they had discussed all of these concerns, the second draft of the contract was completed for everyone to review. It looked like this:

CONTRACT

Effective Dates: December 15 to January 15
We, the undersigned, agree to the following terms:

If Jeff comes home by 9:00 P.M. (or at a different time, if agreed
upon by Jeff and at least one parent) on a school night (Sunday
through Thursday), or by 11:00 P.M. on a weekend night (Friday
or Saturday),
> *Then his parents will let him stay out until 11:30 P.M. one*
> *weekend night a week.*

If Jeff does his own laundry,
> *Then Beverly will iron his school clothes.*

If Jeff completes his homework each night that he has home-
work (and Jeff's word will be taken as to whether or not he has
homework),
> *Then his parents will give him an allowance of $10.00 a*
> *week.*

If Jeff talks to both parents in a respectful manner (which
means no sarcasm, swearing, name calling, or using an
unfriendly tone),
> *Then his parents will allow him to have friends visit him*
> *at home (as long as one parent is home) without criticiz-*
> *ing them.*

Bonus: If Jeff achieves all A and B grades on his report card,
> *then his parents will give him a bonus of $25.00 which he*
> *can spend in any way he chooses.*
Penalty: For every class Jeff cuts or misses without excuse, he
> *will forfeit one dollar ($1.00) from his allowance.*
Anytime Mr. Walters swears at Jeff or calls Jeff a name, a dollar
> *($1.00) will be added to Jeff's allowance for that week.*

The Final Draft of a Contract

There were just a few rough spots to smooth out after this second draft. Actually, given the number of problems the family had had in the past, the discussions about contract terms were going quite well.

It was relatively easy for them to make some minor changes in the contract. For instance, some definitions still needed work. Jeff's parents were still not sure they could trust him to do his homework on his own if they didn't check with him every night. Jeff wasn't clear about what "talking to both parents in a respectful manner" was and wasn't. When those parts of the contract were ironed out, everyone agreed they would try it and see what happened.

That's when they made a copy for each party and everyone signed the contracts at the same time. Now the importance of the effective date would become apparent. Usually, it is better to specify a short period of time to try the contract out (the Walterses opted for one month). At the end of the time period, the family should meet to make sure it is working the way they hoped it would and to make any needed revisions.

Often, before even a couple of weeks are up, problems arise that no one expected. These can usually be worked out fairly easily, but sometimes new negotiations have to be opened up and a new draft of the contract is required (along with a new signing and the discarding of the old contract).

If the whole process works the way it is supposed to, the family finds new ways of talking to each other and working out problems. Sometimes they can't do this on their own, and it may be necessary to work with a psychotherapist or family counselor. But if it is possible to discuss the provisions of a contract, write several drafts of a contract, and jointly come up with a workable document, in most cases the family is well on its way toward a better way of resolving problems. Ultimately, this should result in more consistent use of Rewards, Privileges, and Punishments with children and adolescents. That will result in improved behavior.

This is exactly what happened in Jeff Walters' family. Not all of his parents' initial complaints or concerns were addressed in the contract. Nonetheless, the process of discussing and putting together a contract opened up greater communication. Jeff felt he could talk about things that bothered him about family life. His father and stepmother believed they had better control over him, that he was trying to get along, and that he was not being defiant or trying to get them angry.

Summary

A contract is a written agreement that provides for acceptable behavior change in a child or adolescent. It is best used after other discipline methods and approaches have been tried and found not to work well, and when the misbehavior is fairly serious.

The parents and the young person must meet to begin discussing what should go in the contract. The contract will specify who does what, when, and how, and it tells what each person in the family gets for doing certain things.

As with any agreement or contract, one between children and parents must be negotiated freely and openly. An agreement must be reached without the young person feeling coerced into accepting any provision of the contract.

Both parents and child have an opportunity to express grievances, and getting grievances out in the open for discussion is essential.

In the contract, definitions of behavior to be changed or monitored must be specific and clear so that there is no ambiguity about whether the terms of the contract are being met or violated.

Spell out the rewards and privileges the parents will grant to help provide motivation for the young person to change behavior.

Specify an effective starting and ending date. The contract should be in effect for a relatively short period of time so that it can be monitored, revised, or changed as needed. If someone can think of a way to improve it, rewrite the contract.

Finally, it's important to emphasize again that no one—neither a child nor a parent—should be forced into accepting a contract. It will not work unless there is agreement on all terms. Only when all parties have agreed to all terms should the contract be signed.

Following is a sample contract that you can fill in to use in your family. Be sure to read this chapter and the summary carefully before beginning to use this method of changing behavior.

CONTRACT

Effective Dates: From —————— *to* —————— .

We, the undersigned parties, agree to perform the following:

If ——————————————————————————
Then ——————————————————————————

If ——————————————————————————
Then ——————————————————————————

If ——————————————————————————
Then ——————————————————————————

Bonus: ——————————————————————————
Penalty: ——————————————————————————

Signatures:

——————————————————————————
——————————————————————————
——————————————————————————

13.

Using ESCAPE to Handle

Out-of-Control Children

Negotiating a contract can work with many children and adolescents. But some are so out of control that solutions must go beyond a contract. Parents of these children usually readily admit that normal discipline techniques aren't going to work and that extreme measures must be taken.

That's where Advanced Discipline can be the salvation of a family. And beyond Contracting there is ESCAPE.

ESCAPE is an acronym that stands for:

Escape from old ways
Structure a new program in which privileges must be earned
Create a list of rules your child is expected to follow
Assess all of the privileges extended to your child
Plan an accounting system for earning credits
Exchange privileges for credits earned by following rules

Usually, the kind of extreme measures represented by Contracting and ESCAPE are required when a young person is virtually running his or her parents' and his or her own life without regard for anyone else's feelings, comforts, or property—or when parents feel they have lost all control, and fear for their safety or the safety of the young person. When the child (ESCAPE has been used with children as young as eight years old) or teen calls the shots, orders the parents around, refuses to contribute to the family, and gives every indication of planning to continue to do what he or she wants, when he or she wants, and how he or she wants, Advanced Discipline is an appropriate approach.

Jennifer Williams fits this description. At fifteen, she told her mother what she would and wouldn't do. She left home when she wanted to and returned when—or if—she chose.

"I scream, rant, and rave at her," said Joan Williams, Jennifer's mother. "I know I become unglued about her, but there's no recourse. She lies all the time and comes home when she feels like it. She's in trouble at school and never brings schoolwork home. If I ask her about school, she screams at me, as if I didn't have a right to talk to her about school."

Jennifer had hit her mother on several occasions and called her degrading names. The girl refused to do chores and behaved as though her mother owed it to her to do her laundry, make meals, and buy her things. Jennifer basically used her home as a place to sleep when she got tired and to eat when she was hungry.

Jennifer never seemed to have a decent word to say to her mother, except at times when she wanted something—like money. If her mother asked her for some help with the chores, Jennifer told her, without hesitation or guilt, where she could go. Requesting that Jennifer be a part of the family, follow rules, or accept routines was out of the question. "F— you!" was a standard answer from Jennifer.

If Joan tried to enforce a rule, set a limit, or impose a standard, Jennifer defied her. If Joan tried to physically block her from leaving the house, Jennifer would hit her or push her aside. Joan was frustrated, and believed that the only choice left to her was to turn Jennifer over to the juvenile court authorities or send her to an institution for delinquent and troubled girls. "I wonder if there is any hope for her," she said desperately at one point.

Jennifer seemed to fit the definition of "troubled." She was oppositional and defiant at home, incorrigible in her actions toward her mother, and a troublemaker at school (where she cut classes and treated her teachers much as she treated her mother). She engaged in delinquent behavior such as running away, shoplifting, and drinking with older friends.

Then, Joan Williams heard about ESCAPE in one of my 8-week parent-training programs. She was willing to give it a try.

She realized that she had long ago lost control of her daughter and that her own inability to be firm, to be consistent, to set and enforce limits, and to discipline in effective ways had led to a situation in which she had an unruly child whose behavior she could no longer hope to monitor. Using firm control was out of the question, because she had no control at all. Much of the problem—and she could admit this—stemmed from her practice of some of the worst parenting habits. Yet she said she felt powerless to overcome them.

These ineffective parenting habits included picking at Jennifer and constantly berating her for her poor behavior and attitude. She also resorted to begging Jennifer to straighten up, promising her compensation, and giving her whatever she wanted, hoping against hope that this would lead her daughter to treat her better. "I know I take all this personally," lamented Joan. "But I feel tortured by her behavior. This is my only child, and I want her to do well in life. But I don't know how to help her."

When I explained ESCAPE to her, Joan said she would do anything if she could help her daughter straighten up. I told her, though, that it would be hard. She would be required to maintain her high motivation, stick to the approach, and stop making some earlier mistakes. I also told her that this time it would be easier, because in this Advanced Discipline program I would spell out each step of the way for her.

Starting ESCAPE: Establishing Rules

A premise of ESCAPE is that even when young people are badly out of control, making poor decisions, and failing to obey their parents, they still get pretty much what they want. That is, parents are so used to meeting their kids' needs that young people don't have to behave well in order to go on very comfortably with their lives.

For their parents, giving to them—and giving in to their demands—is a way of life. They wouldn't dream of cutting off the supply of money, clothes, TVs, stereos, CDs, transportation, privileges, and extras that most 1990s kids come to expect.

ESCAPE recognizes this fact of contemporary life, while also understanding that often the breakdown of contemporary families leads parents to these excesses. Instead of helping their children learn to be responsible and appropriately independent, they are reinforcing in those kids dependency, constant handouts, and irresponsibility.

Advanced Discipline in general, and ESCAPE in particular, holds that kids are not entitled to unconditional love and excesses. They must earn love, affection, parental approval, and the myriad of good things parents work hard to provide for their children.

When parents clearly understand these initial premises, they are ready to begin the ESCAPE program. But parents who want to try this approach must be prepared to say good-bye to giving their kids an unconditional taste of the good life.

To start operation ESCAPE, decide on a few basic rules you would like your child to follow. At most there should be five or six such rules. Here are the rules the parents of fourteen-year-old Kevin chose when he returned from a psychiatric treatment center following home truancy, alcohol use, and disobedience:

Rule 1: Kevin will show respect and obedience to his parents by—

A. Treating them with the respect due parents;
B. Not yelling, swearing, or being uncontrolled in anger directed at his parents;
C. Not lying to his parents;
D. Obeying the reasonable requests of his parents.

Rule 2: Kevin will let his parents know where he is going and when he will return at all times by—

A. Asking permission before he leaves home;
B. Coming home directly from school;
C. Telling his parents always where he will be;
D. Calling to tell his parents when he will not be where he said he would be.

Rule 3: Kevin will attend school every day without missing, cutting, or skipping any classes.

Rule 4: Kevin will complete his duties, responsibilities, and assigned chores daily by—

A. Going to bed at 9:00 P.M. on school nights;
B. Going to his tutor once a week;
C. Vacuuming the house and taking out the trash on Monday, Wednesday, and Saturday by 5:00 P.M.
D. Spending at least one hour on homework on Sunday, Monday, Tuesday, Wednesday, Thursday, and Friday, between the hours of 4:00 P.M. and 8:00 P.M.

Setting rules such as the ones that Kevin's parents set for him is an integral part of the program and a logical starting point for this type of discipline. In well-functioning families there is a set of rules, although sometimes they are not formally discussed or written down. Most families need the structure of an explicit set of rules and procedures. If things have gotten out of hand with a young person, it may be because there is not enough structure to guide the child's life.

In almost every family in which there are severe behavior problems, parents are arguing too much with their acting-out kids about rules and behavior. Writing down explicit rules in the form of a contract, as described in the last chapter, should lead to fewer arguments. Such an approach is a first step for weaker or more permissive parents who have to learn how to enforce rules.

Some Rules Parents May Consider for Use in ESCAPE

- Show respect to parents and other family members
- Let parents know whereabouts at all times
- Attend school regularly
- Return home by an agreed-on curfew
- Complete home chores
- Attend to personal hygiene
- Refrain from alcohol and drug use
- Follow established rules in family
- Express anger in appropriate ways

Starting with these rules lets a child or teen know exactly what the parents expect. Because they are written down and spelled out in detail, there should be no need to question them. If any question or ambiguity arises, then the rules can be amended to be more accurate or more clearly stated.

Listing All the Privileges Given to Your Child

Once you've made the list of rules, the second step is to decide the privileges that are given or extended to your child. It is important to make an extensive list of everything you do for your kid.

Here's the list Joan Williams made for her daughter Jennifer:

I allow her to:
Use the telephone
Get an allowance
Go out with her friends
Have friends come over to visit
Have friends stay overnight

Use the family motorcycle
Have lunch money for school
Buy clothes for school and play
Get haircuts and perms
Buy toiletries
Have money for tickets to concerts
Use the family car
Pick out paint and wallpaper for her room
Attend summer camp
Watch television in the family room
Go to dinner with mother
Attend movies with mother

Having made a comprehensive list of nearly everything (if not everything) your child gets free by living in your house, you're ready to figure out how she can earn all these wonderful fringe benefits.

To do this requires some simple math. It may seem complicated at first, but it is well worth the effort in the long run.

How Your Child Will Earn Privileges

Figure out a system for how your child earns privileges. Obviously, your child will earn privileges by following the rules, but it's more complicated than that. You'll need to assign a dollar or point value to both the rules to follow and the privileges to earn. Your child must accumulate so many points or dollars (you may like the idea of using coupons or play money) in order to "buy" privileges. By following the rules, your child earns points (dollars, coupons, credits, etc.), which can be exchanged for privileges.

Kevin's parents decided on this accounting system:

Kevin could earn dollar credits by following all the rules every day. If he followed each rule, each day, he would earn $240.00 in credit a week or $40.00 a day. (Note: This is not given to him as real money, but as coupons or as an amount written on a card or piece of paper.)

His privileges would "cost" him the following:

1. Use of telephone—incoming or outgoing calls: $1.00 per call.
2. Allowance: $10.00 a week ($10.00 credit exchanged for $10.00 real cash).
3. Going out with a friend on one day or one evening: $10.00.
4. Having a friend come over when parents are home and give permission: $5.00.
5. Use of his motor scooter: $15.00 a day.
6. Lunch money for school: $2.00 a day ($2.00 credit exchanged for $2.00 cash).
7. New clothes or shoes: one-third of actual cost (example: Kevin must turn in coupons worth $30.00 for parents to buy a $90.00 pair of shoes).
8. Haircuts: $12.00 (coupons exchanged for equivalent cash).
9. Ticket for a concert: $20.00 (coupons exchanged for equivalent cash).
10. Being able to pick out wallpaper or paint: $50.00.
11. Attending basketball camp: $125.00.

How the Program Operates

Once parents have drawn up the list of rules and figured out an accounting system, they set down on paper the rules of the program. This is to help them fully understand it themselves and be able to present something in writing to their child.

The rules of the program might be drafted in this manner (using Kevin as an illustration):

- There are four basic rules for Kevin to follow (See Rules Sheet).

- If Kevin follows all parts of all four rules every day, he earns $40.00 in credit for that day.
- The $40.00 credit will be given to Kevin on a slip of paper signed by one parent. This will be given by 11:00 P.M. each day.
- When a rule or any part of a rule is broken, Kevin is to be notified of this in writing by 11:00 P.M. of each day. There will be no discussion of the breaking of rules.
- For Kevin to be able to use or have any privilege, he must turn in a credit coupon to one parent, who will verify that he has enough credit available for that privilege. There is to be no discussion beyond whether or not Kevin has enough credit in his possession. There are no advances or extensions of credit!
- If Kevin keeps all rules for seven straight days, he can earn a bonus of $20.00 in credit.
- Kevin cannot go to any other family member, friend, or relative to earn extra money, borrow credit, or get around this program.

Presenting the Program to the Child

Everything about the program so far is to be worked out by the parent in preparation for telling the child. Unlike making a contract, which involves discussion and negotiation, ESCAPE assumes that the child is too far out of control to be considered a partner in righting things at this point. The parent or parents alone must work out the whole system, put it in writing, and then arrange for a meeting with the child.

In such a meeting, the parent can make a short statement that goes something like this:

"Jonathan, I've been increasingly concerned about the way we've been getting along. We're fighting and arguing too much, and this bothers me, just as I think it probably bothers you. I've come up with a plan to help us cut down on the problems in this family.

"I think if I yell at you less, you'll like it better. I know I yell too much. On the other hand, I'd like it better if you obeyed me and followed some of my rules. So I've come up with a program that will help us accomplish these things. Here, take a look at these rules and the way the program operates."

That's generally the best way for parents to present ESCAPE to their kids—not focusing on how bad the child is, but putting more emphasis on mutual problems they have and suggesting that they, as parents, bear as much responsibility for what is going wrong as do kids.

Now, how do kids react to this?

Having been present many times when the program and the rules are presented to young people, I can tell you that the reaction is anything but welcome.

Michael, a fifteen-year-old who was used to getting his own way, tore up the rules and the outline of the program and threw the scraps of paper in his parents' face. "I'm not doing it!" he shouted. "I do what I want, and you're not telling me what to do!"

Josh, a sixteen-year-old with a swagger and a quick temper, was flabbergasted. "You've got to be kidding!" he said. "Do you think you can make me follow your dumb rules? You can forget that!"

Jennifer, the girl who walked all over her mother, threw the rules on the floor and screamed: "You can take your rules and go to hell! You aren't changing things. I'm the boss here—not you!"

All of these reactions are typical and expected, and parents must be prepared for a loud, angry child. But how do parents best handle these kinds of reactions?

First, have plenty of copies of the rules and the program in reserve. Second, be calm, because ultimately you are in control of what happens.

Your response can be something like this: "I'm sorry that you haven't taken the time to look this over. There are other copies, and any time you want to read it over so you know exactly what's happening, let me know. Anyway, the program goes into effect tomorrow morning."

At this time, it doesn't matter whether they like it or dislike it; whether they decide to try to go along with it or not. You will control all of their privileges. If they would like to risk surviving without privileges, it is up to them.

Putting It into Effect

Once it's in effect, you must follow the rules exactly as indicated. There is to be no yelling, reminding, nit-picking, discussion, threats, or warnings about rules or behavior. Your role is to be aware of any rule that is broken, make a note of it, and by the designated time each day indicate on paper (or on an index card, which works very well) whether it's a hit or miss—that is, whether your child followed all the rules and thus earns credit for that day, or broke one or more rules and therefore loses credit for the day.

Usually it's best to put the card or paper indicating a hit or a miss in the same place every day at the same time. Some parents post it on a bulletin board, slip it under their kid's bedroom door, place it on a dresser, or tape it to a bedroom door. What is required is that you, as the parent, avoid discussing and arguing about the breaking of a rule.

You can use all the Praise and Attention you want when your child keeps the rules and does well.

Kids who are determined to break the system may hold out for a few days or even a week. Eventually, most have no choice. If they want the privileges and fringe benefits of the life they've become used to, they must give in and go along with the program.

The hard part for parents is to hang in there in the beginning when a young person hopes to regain control by trying to subvert and disrupt the parental effort to assert control.

Consistency and firmness are imperative. Some young people will try to negotiate or talk you out of it with promises and bribes. This is probably what got you into difficulty in the first place, so you cannot give in to such tactics when initiating this program.

As I said, most come around. And in fact, when parents show they are consistent, and stop yelling or talking about misbehavior and broken rules, children and adolescents not only come around, but they *like* the program. I have heard young people say it was a neat program and easy to follow. "I get more things now than I ever got," Josh said, "and no one is yelling at me." The benefit for Josh's parents was that Josh was doing all the things they wanted from him. When he didn't, he was the first to acknowledge it. Finally, he knew exactly what the consequences were, and he liked the absence of any arbitrariness in the rules and consequences from his parents.

What Can Go Wrong?

A couple of things can spell defeat for ESCAPE. One is that you have a child or teenager so determined not to give in to following rules that he or she runs away or tries to find another place to live. Such a drastic response on the part of a young person can actually be helpful to parents. If kids go to live with a friend, find a runaway shelter, or go to a relative's house, they will encounter rules and structure. If they end up in a psychiatric hospital or an institution that caters to minors, again there are definite rules young people have to follow to earn privileges and status.

Since they have little choice, and such a program is carried out in a rather dispassionate fashion in the hospital, a runaway shelter, or an institution, kids become used to it. On returning home, they are more accustomed to the type of structure their parents have in mind. Consequently, one way or another, their resistance to going along with ESCAPE is usually short-lived, and the program can be enacted when they arrive back home.

When Kevin got out of the psychiatric hospital, the program was in place and waiting for his return. On arriving home, he was willing to accept a new program because he had gotten used to more structure and rules in the hospital. Kids who run away usually are ready to accept some changes when they return home. Life on the road, with friends, or with relatives is usually not half as pleasant as life at home.

The other thing that can go wrong is . . . you!

The fact is, I have never seen a child scuttle one of these programs. I think most of them come to appreciate the predictability and the common sense of the contingent privileges. But in every ESCAPE program I've witnessed in which there were serious problems, those difficulties were due to parent lapses.

Parents can insure the failure of any discipline program by failing to follow the rules of the program. They do this by returning to old ways of handling problems—yelling, using threats, or resorting to discipline methods other than the ones prescribed.

They can also bring about failure by either not honoring the child's request when it comes time to cash in points or coupons earned for a privilege, or by cashing in points or coupons before they were earned. Or they can allow a child to have advance credit, to operate on a promise, or to break a rule without losing points, perhaps because they feel guilty about instituting or maintaining this kind of program.

Once a parent has allowed the program to get out of control, no child is going to go back on it voluntarily and have to earn privileges once again. There have been cases, though, when kids have been angry with their parents for failing to follow the rules and have stuck to ESCAPE themselves long after their parents quit using it.

But when parents persistently stick to the program and see it through the early struggles of learning to be more consistent, structured, and in-control, the benefits are worth it. Joan Williams found this out with Jennifer. The program stopped arguments and led to a much better-behaved daughter who began to follow rules and treat her mother with respect.

A few months after the program started, Joan reported that she and Jennifer were actually having fun together, and arguments like the ones that used to take place had stopped. "My daughter knows what will happen if she comes home late or lies to me," Joan said. "Usually she tells me what my response will be before I have a chance to—and we're like a real family, finally."

Summary

The steps to using the Advanced Discipline technique of ESCAPE are as follows:

1. **Make a short set of rules (no more than six) for your child; write this list down and make the rules as clear and as explicit as possible.**
2. **Make a complete list of what you provide and do for your child.**
3. **Figure out a system of how your child can earn privileges on a daily basis.**
4. **Sit down with your child and tell your child about your feelings about a need to make changes in the family. The explanation should include the following points:**
   - **You are upset about the problems in the family.**
   - **There is too much yelling, fighting, and arguing.**
   - **You have contributed to the problems.**
   - **You would like to change yourself as well as assist your child to change.**
5. **Present your child with a copy of the rules.**
6. **Indicate exactly when the plan goes into effect.**
7. **Keep up your end of the bargain by doing all those parts of the program that require effort on your part. They include:**
   - **Indicate in writing each day at a certain time whether your child has earned points or credit by following all the rules or lost all credit for that day by having broken at least one rule.**
   - **Do not talk about broken rules. The only exceptinions that you can confirm that a certain rule was bro-**

ken ("Yes, that's right. You broke rule number four by coming home late").

• **When credits or points have been earned, make it possible for your child to use or spend those points or credits.**

• **Do not remind, criticize, warn, or threaten about the possibility of your child's breaking a rule.**

• **Do not add any new rules or change any other part of the program unless it is necessary for the survival of the program.**

You may use the following outline to create an ESCAPE program for your home.

ESCAPE WORKSHEET

I. Start by making a list of rules for your child.
Rule 1: ———————————————————
————————————————————————

Rule 2: ———————————————————
————————————————————————

Rule 3: ———————————————————
————————————————————————

Rule 4: ———————————————————
———————————————————————— .

II. List all the things you provide or give to your child in the following categories:
A. Privileges:
1: ———————————————————————
————————————————————————

2: ———————————————————————
————————————————————————

3: ———————————————————————
————————————————————————

4: _____

5: _____

Other: _____

B. *Money, Allowance, or Payments:*

1: _____

2: _____

3: _____

4: _____

5: _____

Other: _____

C. *Material Possessions:*

1: _____

2: _____

3: _____

4: _____

5: _____

Other: _____

D. *Other Fringe Benefits Provided by Parents:*

1: _____

_____

2: _____

_____

3: _____

_____

4: _____

_____

5: _____

_____

III. Determine a system for how your child will earn privileges and how you will keep track of the earning and buying of privileges:

A. Figure out an accounting system that suits you.

B. Figure out how you and your child will keep track of points or credits earned and spent.

IV. Make a list of the rules of the program. These rules will be written out and presented to your child along with the set of rules and the privileges that can be earned.

V. Make a list of the points you want to make when you tell your child about the program for the first time.

A: _____

_____

B: _____

_____

C: _____

_____

D: _____

_____

E: _____

_____

VI. Pick the dates you will tell your child about the program and the official starting date of the program:

A. Date to tell child: _____

_____

B. Date to start program: _____

_____

14.

10 Steps to Maintaining Better Behavior

Now that your child is better behaved and you are feeling good about both yourself and your youngster, it's time to go over some things that will both help your child maintain the improvement and help you continue to be a better parent.

As part of this final chapter, it is useful to revisit the steps for more effective parenting, and to add several other dimensions to what you need to know and do to be the kind of parent who can handle problems as they come along.

In Chapter 4 (Week 1) we covered the 12 Keys to Effective Parenting. They are:

- Providing love, affection, and concern
- Helping children build self-esteem
- Having respect for children
- Accepting children and showing approval
- Having a good understanding of discipline techniques
- Providing clear and reasonable expectations
- Being consistent in handling children
- Setting strict and firm limits
- Having consistent parenting approaches among all the child-care figures in the home
- Enforcing limits
- Allowing dissent and expression of feelings within the limits
- Being able to let go of our children

One way of maintaining your child's acceptable and desired behavior is to remind yourself frequently of these 12 essential keys to effective parenting. Many of these points have been touched on in this book so far. A few have not, and I would like to mention them right now.

Respecting Our Children

What does respecting our children mean?

To me it means viewing them as people with rights and always remembering that they are human beings capable of thinking, feeling, and making judgments commensurate with their age and developmental level. Children are entitled to love, care, concern, and protection. They have a right to express their feelings and to be treated with dignity. They should be considered growing individuals who learn from experience, require sensitive and responsive handling, need love, and have the capacity for ideas, thoughts, and desires worthy of consideration.

The parent who treats a child respectfully listens to the child's point of view, treats the child as a worthwhile person, and does not degrade the child by hitting, belittling, or shouting. Children who are given respect are included in a growing number of decisions as they develop and are told that their ideas are worthwhile.

Allowing Dissent and Expression

Another important tool for being an effective parent is to allow dissent and expression of feelings within limits. Children cannot just be "seen and not heard." For them to grow up healthy and strong, they must be allowed to express feelings, but always within certain limits.

It was fashionable years ago—perhaps it still is in some families—to allow children complete freedom so that they will grow up uninhibited. This permissiveness sounded good on paper, and it made for some compelling books about childrearing (such as A. S. Neill's *Summerhill*), but in truth it has not worked out very well. Limits and rules provide guidelines for children, and those who grow up without them, studies have shown, are not as well adjusted as children who are provided very definite limits.

Within limits and rules, children can be free to express opinions and feelings, and whatever they express should be accepted and respected. Children have the right to their feelings, and should be encouraged to voice those feelings. They do not, on the other hand, have the right to tyrannize their parents and others in the name of "just being honest."

Letting Go of Our Children

The title of one parenting book expresses a most important principle of effective parenting. The book, written by Richard Robertiello in 1975, is *Hold Them Very Close, Then Let Them Go.* That is essentially what parents should do.

In the early years, we must hold children close, develop a secure relationship with them, make sure they feel loved, and give them a lot of warmth and protection. Then, having accomplished this, we must gradually let go.

Ultimately, we must help them to be independent and self-sufficient. In order for children to be healthy and well-functioning adults, they have to be able to live on their own and support themselves. Our childrearing tactics and discipline strategies should always be based on this goal, and we should constantly ask ourselves, Will what I'm doing help my child to be more independent, secure, and self-sufficient?

Impatient parents often have difficulty with this issue. It's not that they want to make their children dependent—they just want things to be done right and quickly.

A successful engineer once told me that he had trouble with teaching independence. "I get impatient," he said, "if they don't do it right now. I get tired and fed up with their efforts, and I tell them to get out of here and let me do it. So then I do what they should have done. I know that's not good for them."

Letting go means giving children more responsibility, demanding more from them, allowing them to try new things (and occasionally make mistakes as they do), and granting increasing independence as we trust them more.

The 10 Steps of Maintaining Better Behavior

In addition to the 12 Keys to Effective Parenting, there are some other aspects of parenting and discipline that are important in the care and maintenance of well-behaved children. I call these the 10 Steps to Maintaining Better Behavior.

Step 1. Be aware of how you achieved improved behavior with your child and pledge not to slip back into old patterns of parenting behavior.

I know this is easier said than done. But it is also true that if you have corrected some previously faulty ways of dealing with your child and you like the results, you must work hard at making sure both you and your youngster don't regress to behavior that wasn't working so well before.

Maybe this means that you have to monitor yourself closely, or enlist the assistance of a spouse or friend. Sometimes having an agreement with another adult about letting you know when you've reverted to ineffective discipline methods can be helpful. Often, though, we can take cues from our children.

What they do (such as returning to old misbehavior) or say ("Why are you always yelling at me?") can serve as a good indication that we need to make a quick reversal in how we're handling the parenting job.

Certainly it will be helpful to evaluate yourself periodically to see how you are measuring up on your own personal Parenting

Competence Questionnaire. If you don't rate very high, then maybe it's time to reread parts of this book or redouble efforts to stay on course with discipline that works.

Step 2. Work on keeping your stress level manageable and get help if you're depressed.

As I wrote in Chapter 2 ("Why Do Children Develop Behavior Problems"), both parental stress and parental depression can significantly affect your ability to apply the discipline techniques discussed in this book effectively. When you're too highly stressed or have sunk into a gloomy or depressive state, you are not likely to be able to deal well with your children, let alone with the other important things in life.

The problem, though, is that stress and depression are often insidious, creeping up on us before we are fully aware of how much of a grip they have on us. If you are a single parent without close cooperation or a "consulting" relationship with another adult, then you could be vulnerable to allowing various mental or emotional conditions to take over.

I have found again and again in my parenting groups that one of the most significant benefits of having parents get together is that they are able to learn more about themselves in a group setting. In a parenting workshop, they begin to see themselves as others see them. That means that the group holds up a mirror for them to see their own reflection. The group helps them to better recognize how stressed, depressed, lonely, or isolated they are. In the 8 weeks of a parenting course, a mother or father can feel less alone and find adult contacts who add pleasure and sociability to their lives.

After the 8-week program is over, many parents keep in touch with the others they've met and usually sense their need for an ongoing support group. If you find yourself too lonely, isolated, and cut off from other adults who can help to lift you out of sadness or depression, consider finding a parenting support group where you can talk about parenting and personal issues as often as needed.

Better-Behavior Maintenance Checklist for Parents

Answer each of the following questions by circling the number that best corresponds to your honest reply. If most of your answers are "3," you're doing well in maintaining a well-behaved child.

If you have some answers that are "1," you need to work on those areas of parenting.

1	2	3
Never	Sometimes	Always

1. My rules are predictable from day to day.   1 2 3
2. The way I respond to problems with my child is basically consistent and is not dependent on my moods.   1 2 3
3. When I give my child a punishment, I don't back down and change it.   1 2 3
4. I give compliments and praise to my child more than once a day.   1 2 3
5. I expect my child to be responsible.   1 2 3
6. I keep requests and commands simple and direct. 1 2 3
7. I state commands and requests only once.   1 2 3
8. I always know where my child is and what he or she is doing.   1 2 3

Step 3. Communicate openly with your children.

When things go wrong in families, it's often because communication has been disrupted in some way. Much of discipline has to do with effective communication—perhaps the most important key to helping children learn responsible behavior. If you cannot communicate well with children, the principles you want them to learn may not be clear to them.

In fact, the art of communication is both the sending and receiving of messages that have meaning to both parties in a transaction.

**Better-Behavior Maintenance Checklist
for Parents** (cont.)

9. I have just a few rules and my child knows and understands them.   *1 2 3*

10. I encourage my child to express his or her point of view.   *1 2 3*

11. I am willing to hold firm to a demand or expectation even if this results in a conflict with my child.   *1 2 3*

12. I encourage my child to make decisions.   *1 2 3*

13. I try to understand my child's wishes and feelings.   *1 2 3*

14. I encourage my child to appreciate and talk about his or her accomplishments.   *1 2 3*

15. I actively and purposely teach my child how to solve problems.   *1 2 3*

16. I plan time each day to spend with my child.   *1 2 3*

17. I show respect to my child by listening, being respectful, never using sarcasm and put-downs, and being courteous.   *1 2 3*

18. I always take time to show interest in my child and his or her activities, friends, and plans.   *1 2 3*

19. I ask for my child's ideas, suggestions, and thoughts.   *1 2 3*

20. I try to do at least one thing each day to build my child's self-esteem.   *1 2 3*

There are many ways to communicate with children—through gestures, signals, and other actions. However, the best and most common way to communicate is through well-chosen words. When words are not simple, direct, and clear, the message is often lost.

I was listening to a father and his teenage daughter, Felicia, trying to talk to each other one day. Their conversation, in part, went something like this:

Felicia: Why don't you just send me to a boarding school?

Father: I looked into it and decided not to.

Felicia: You looked into it? Ha! You glanced at a book.

Father: Yes, I did look at the book about boarding schools.

Felicia: But did you call any? No!

Father: No, I didn't. But I know they are too expensive and too far away.

Felicia: In other words, you don't want me to go to a good school.

Father: No, that's not it.

Felicia: What is it?

Father: You would have the same problems no matter where you go.

Felicia: "No I wouldn't."

Father: You don't mind giving up your friends and your sports to go to a boarding school. That sounds like a problem to me.

Felicia: Maybe it does to you. You're the one I have a problem with. You don't like me and you want to get rid of me. So just send me away.

Father: That's not the way you solve problems.

Felicia: Well, it's obvious we can't solve problems in other ways. I can't talk to you.

Father: You don't listen.

Felicia: You're stubborn and cruel and an asshole.

Father: See what I mean? You think going to a boarding school is going to solve your problem with sarcasm and disrespect to adults? You swear at me all the time.

Felicia: I do not.

This wasn't the end of the conversation, but I think you can get the drift. This father and daughter had poor communication with each other. Neither seemed to be truly listening to the other. They just picked up on words that the other said in order to send them back, often in the form of an accusation. They asked questions not to gain information but to make comments, and did not expect an answer. They did not understand each other's point of view, and it was clear that compromise was an art neither practiced well. To communicate better, Felicia and her father would have to learn to listen to each other, respect each other's feelings, and accept each other's ideas as valid.

While exchanging information, stating rules, and defining expectations are important functions of communication, there are other ways communication works in families. It can be useful to clear the air over an issue or to settle thorny problems that have a lot of emotion attached to them. Communication is absolutely essential in problem solving.

To keep a child behaving better, you must model good communication skills while teaching your children about effective communication.

Step 4. Be a role model for your children.

Is this the single most vital part of parenting? I don't know whether it is, but I do know it is a significant part of being a competent mother or father. Parents teach not only by what they say but also by who they are and what they do. Parents must always remember that their actions are like billboards sending messages directly to children. The message is: This is the way people in this family behave.

Imitation of our behavior and actions is one of the powerful ways children learn from us, and its importance should not be underestimated. Through imitative learning children find out who they are and what pleases the people with whom they identify. While early imitative learning has to do with identity, children also begin to figure out which behaviors are considered good and bad. Through watching, observing, and imitating mother and father, children learn what is proper behavior.

Most parents realize early on in raising a child that it's not advisable to do some things we did before there were children in the house. We can no longer act any way we'd like to, but must behave in order to properly influence our children. When parents are aware that their behavior is an influence, they can consciously and deliberately choose to act in ways that teach and guide children to imitate responsible or "good" behavior.

For instance, by communicating well with each other, parents can teach communication skills and demonstrate the importance of talking out problems and exchanging information. By making appropriate decisions and letting kids know how they reached those decisions, parents teach about decision-making. By modeling healthy behavior (e.g., not smoking, not using alcohol or drugs, exercising regularly, eating healthy foods), parents again are teaching by example.

Step 5. Be closely involved with your children.

In order to be an effective role model for your kids to imitate, you must be a positive and powerful figure in their life. Not only must you communicate well, but you must be involved in their life.

Surveys show that time spent with parents is one of the most pleasant memories children have later in life. Doing things together, kids agree, is what makes for happy families. That's why in their book Secrets of Strong Families, authors Nick Stinnett and John DeFrain list time together as one of the secrets of building and maintaining a strong family life.

I have often found that families in which children are acting up and misbehaving seldom set aside planned time for the whole family to be together engaged in fun activities. Only when family members play together, attend church or a synagogue as a family, eat meals together, plan activities, go on vacations, and do the myriad of other things families can do—will a family function well. That is, only by frequent and prolonged involvement can there be communication, problem solving, and ample opportunities for parents to serve as role models.

Step 6. Be responsive to your children.

Being involved in the activities of your child's life is important, but to be involved on an emotional level requires that you be responsive while being together. This is a tall order, particularly if you're not adept at responding to your children in a warm, friendly, understanding manner.

Being responsive means understanding the emotions and needs of children; taking their wishes, feelings, and needs into consideration when making decisions or responding to them; and showing a willingness to cooperate with them.

It's important not only to spend lots of time with children but also to be a warm, caring, sensitive parent during some of that time. Don't just respond to behavior, but also listen to and respond to feelings, needs, wishes, hopes, fears, and dreams.

Being responsive means that you tune in to subtle cues and you show appropriate reactions to a child's behavior and underlying feelings.

Step 7. Monitor and supervise the behavior of your children.

To be an effective and outstanding parent, there is no doubt that you must monitor your child's behavior and actions. Often parents of young people who get into trouble have little idea where their kids are, who they're with, or what they're doing.

Young people of all ages need plenty of supervision. They need to be directed in what they do and have limits firmly set when they are behaving in unacceptable ways.

In describing the Advanced Discipline techniques of Contracting and ESCAPE in Chapters 12 and 13, I emphasized how important it is to have family rules. These should include the requirement that kids obtain permission to go out and let parents know where they're going, who they will be with, and what time they will return. Establishing these kinds of rules early in a youngster's life and maintaining a strict control over them will eliminate problems during the teenage years.

Step 8. Demand mature and responsible behavior from your child.

You should expect mature and compliant behavior. Expect children to do what you ask or demand. Expect that they will act their age—without having to be told to do so. Expect them to be responsible and to live up to rules and obligations.

The goal is to rear children who are responsible and independent. You cannot do this through low-level demands or by allowing children to function at a younger, less responsible age level.

Call it goal setting, demands for responsible behavior, or expectations of growing up, but do ask that they be mature, well-mannered, and age-appropriate in their actions and behavior no matter where they are.

Step 9. Confront your child about behavior when necessary.

Confrontation means letting a child know when you're unhappy with his or her behavior or actions. This unhappiness should be expressed whether it causes a conflict or not. And that's the essence of confrontation.

An effective parent doesn't avoid confrontations just because the child may react in an inappropriate or cross way. Sometimes parents who are intimidated or manipulated by children react in this way. Diana Baumrind, a psychologist at the University of California at Berkeley, has pointed out in recent research that direct confrontation is vital to raising a competent child.

A confrontation does not have to be ugly, loud, or unpleasant. In fact, most effective confrontations are done in calm, quiet ways. Making eye contact with a child and letting a child know how displeased you are about a behavior or how you expect the behavior to change can work very well. For example, suppose your teenager is slipping in his or her efforts to maintain passing grades. You might say: "I've noticed you're not spending as much time with your schoolwork as you used to. Your grades aren't as high this term as they were last. I'd like you to spend more time studying." Similarly, when a rule or agreement has been violated, parents usually need to let a youngster know about it. In confronting a child in such a situation, you can call attention to the problem without being abrasive: "It seems as if you're having trouble remembering to talk out problems instead of hitting your sister."

Parents who avoid confrontations may be weak or passive, or they may dislike confrontations in general. Failing to confront children about their behavior does a disservice to children. It robs them of the opportunity to assess themselves and make changes. Children may also perceive it as a lack of responsiveness or caring on the part of the parent. Loving parents don't allow children to misbehave or act inappropriately without calling attention to it through confrontation.

Step 10. Continue to learn about child discipline.

Don't stop learning just because your child recently began to behave better. Look at parenting as a full-time job requiring constant upgrading in skills and ability. Approach it as you would any other job. If you want to be successful in most jobs, you will learn more than the next person and try to find out as much as you can about the job requirements, new information, and more efficient and successful ways of doing the work.

There are plenty of magazines, books, and newsletters that give valuable information to parents about how to do the job better. A special listing ("For Further Reading") of useful publications follows this chapter.

Summing Up

What I've tried to do in this book is teach you how to handle your children's most challenging behavior by using a combination of discipline techniques. In 8 weeks, if you follow the steps described, you should see noticeable improvements in your child's difficult behavior. In case additional measures are needed to deal with severe behavior problems, I

have described further, more advanced discipline skills for you to put into action.

Finally, I've shared some of my ideas about what makes for effective parenting and the steps to take to maintain better-behaved children.

Now you're on your own, although you can always return to this book or use the many worthwhile books, magazines, and newsletters that are available to mothers and fathers these days.

Good luck and effective parenting.

For Further Reading

Books

Lee Canter and Marlene Canter, *Assertive Discipline for Parents.* Santa Monica, CA: Canter & Associates, 1982.

Lynn Clark, *The Time-Out Solution: A Parent's Guide for Handling Everyday Behavior Problems.* New York: Contemporary Books, 1989.

Don Dinkmeyer, Sr., and Gary D. McKay, *Systematic Training for Effective Parenting: The Parent's Handbook* (2nd Edition.) Circle Pines, MN: American Guidance Service, 1989.

James Dobson, *Dare to Discipline.* Wheaton, IL: Tyndale, 1973.

Fitzhugh Dodson, *How to Parent.* New York: New American Library, 1971.

Rudolf Dreikurs and Vicki Stolz, *Children: The Challenge.* New York: Dutton, 1987.

Lynne S. Dumas, *Talking with Your Child about a Troubled World.* Fawcett/Columbine, 1992.

Stephen Garber, Marianne Garber, and Robyn F. Spizman, *Good Behavior: Over 1200 Sensible Solutions to Your Child's Problems from Birth to Age Twelve.* New York: Villard Books, 1987.

Christopher Green, *Toddler Taming*. New York: Fawcett, 1985.

Mary Sheedy Kurcinka, *Raising Your Spirited Child*. New York: HarperPerennial, 1992.

Thomas Lickona, *Raising Good Children*. New York: Bantam Books, 1985.

John Rosemond, *Six-Point Plan for Raising Happy, Healthy Children*. Kansas City, Missouri: Andrews & McMeel, 1989.

Nancy Samalin, *Loving Your Child Is Not Enough*. New York: Penguin Books, 1987.

Nick Stinnet and John DeFrain, *Secrets of Strong Families*. Boston: Little, Brown and Company, 1985.

Peter Williamson, *Good Kids, Bad Behavior*. New York: Simon & Schuster, 1990.

James Windell, *Discipline: A Sourcebook of 50 Failsafe Techniques for Parents*. New York: Collier, 1991.

Periodicals for Parents

American Baby
475 Park Avenue South
New York, NY 10016

Child
110 Fifth Avenue
New York, NY 10011

Christian Parenting Today
P.O. Box 850
Sisters, OR 97759

Growing Parent
22 North Second Street
Lafayette, IN 47902

Healthy Kids: Birth–3 Years
475 Park Avenue South
New York, NY 10016

Healthy Kids: 4–10 Years
475 Park Avenue South
New York, NY 10016

Living With Children
127 Ninth Avenue North
Nashville, TN 37234

Parenting Magazine
501 Second Street #110
San Francisco, CA 94107

Parents Magazine
685 Third Avenue
New York, NY 10017

Parent and Preschooler
P.O. Box 1851
Garden City, NY 11530

Today's Family
27 Empire Drive
St. Paul, MN 55103

Working Mother Magazine
230 Park Avenue
New York, NY 10169

Index